Guns of the Lincoln County War

Books by Clifford R. Caldwell

A Day's Ride From Here, Volume I: Mountain Home, Texas

A Day's Ride From Here, Volume II: Noxville, Texas

Dead Right: The Lincoln County War

Eternity at the End of a Rope: Executions, Lynchings and Vigilante Justice in Texas, 1819-*

Fort McKavett and Tales of Menard County

Guns of the Lincoln County War

John Simpson Chisum: The Cattle King of the Pecos Revisited*

Old West Tales: Good Men, Bad Men, Lawmen

Robert Kelsey Wylie, Forgotten Cattle King of Texas

Texas Lawmen 1835–1899: The Good and the Bad

Texas Lawmen 1900–1940: The Good and the Bad

*Published by Sunstone Press

Guns
of the
Lincoln County War

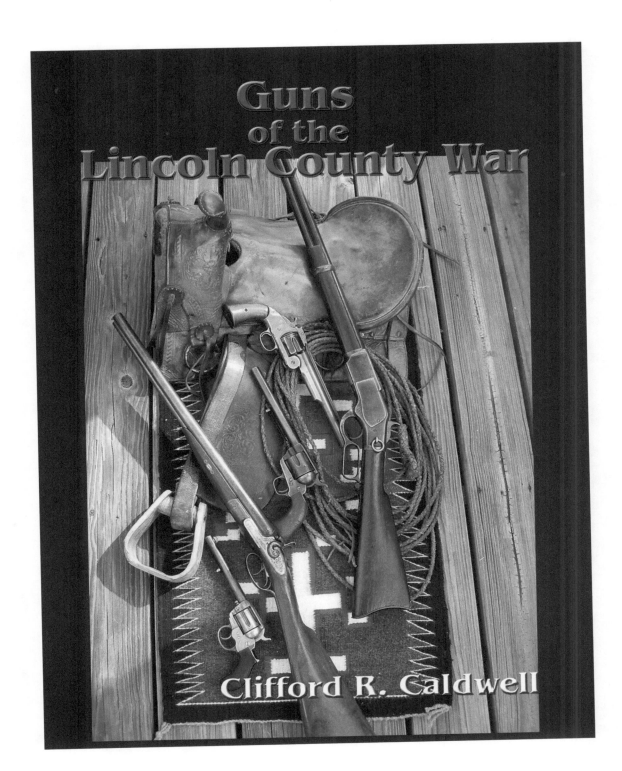

Clifford R. Caldwell

Sunstone
Press

SANTA FE

Note: The information in this book is true and complete to the best of our knowledge. It is offered without guarantee on the part of the author. The author disclaims all liability in connection with the use of this book.

Photographs: Unless otherwise noted, all photographs are the property of the author and are original material of the author. Reproduction of any images without the written permission of the author is prohibited.

Firearms: Unless otherwise noted, all firearms are from the private collection of the author. Reproduction of any images of these firearms without the written permission of the author is prohibited.

Sunstone books may be purchased for educational, business, or sales promotional use. For information please write: Special Markets Department, Sunstone Press, P.O. Box 2321, Santa Fe, New Mexico 87504-2321.

Body typeface › ITC Benguiat Std
Printed on acid-free paper
∞

———————————

Library of Congress Cataloging-in-Publication Data

Names: Caldwell, Clifford R., 1948- author.
Title: Guns of the Lincoln County War / by Clifford R. Caldwell.
Description: Santa Fe, New Mexico : Sunstone Press, [2018] | Previously
    published by Clifford R. Caldwell, 2009. | Includes bibliographical
    references and index.
Identifiers: LCCN 2018052477 | ISBN 9781632932457 (softcover : alk. paper)
Subjects: LCSH: Lincoln County (N.M)–History–19th century. | Firearms–West
    (U.S.)–History–19th century. | Firearms–Design and
    construction–History–19th century. | Gunfights–New Mexico–Lincoln
    County–History–19th century. | Outlaws–West (U.S.)–Biography. | Peace
    officers–West (U.S.)–Biography. | Frontier and pioneer life–West (U.S.)
Classification: LCC F802.L7 C35 2018 | DDC 978.9/64–dc23
LC record available at https://lccn.loc.gov/2018052477

———————————

WWW.SUNSTONEPRESS.COM
SUNSTONE PRESS / POST OFFICE BOX 2321 / SANTA FE, NM 87504-2321 /USA
(505) 988-4418 / ORDERS ONLY (800) 243-5644 / FAX (505) 988-1025

Dedicated to a dear friend,
the best old gun trader there ever was:

Forest Reid McCandless
5 January 1917–2 July 2011

Contents

Foreword

The Lincoln County War in New Mexico has been a passion of mine for many years. Like most, I have read scores of books about this epic battle, and have traveled to the many sites in New Mexico where the fable unfolded. A vast number of authors, researchers and historians have done painstaking research into the accurate portraying the people, places and events of the Lincoln County War none have spent much energy chronicling the firearms used during the conflict. Some years ago I published a book about the saga on the banks of the Rio Bonito titled *Dead Right, The Lincoln County War.* Although my contribution to the ever expanding library of works on the subject does offer some newly discovered information about certain aspects of the story, it too misses the mark in terms of offering the reader a good grounding on the firearms of the period. As I searched through the piles of reference material before me I was amazed that I was unable to find anything credible covering the firearms of the period. More surprising yet was the fact that even less information has been written about the guns used by the significant participants in the conflict.

As a historian I was perhaps more perplexed by the fact that while doing research I encountered numerous artifacts housed in public and private museums and collections whose label made the lofty claim that they were authentic, and that the item had once belonged to Billy the Kid or some other noteworthy participant in the Lincoln County War. In reality, little that I found was legitimate. I was dumb struck by the fact that some of the items were blatantly falsified. Although a firearms expert could decipher what firearms were available to the combatants during the era, and what would constitute an authentic example, it would be a hit and miss proposition at best for someone not well grounded in the history of period firearms.Sufficiently motivated and armed with the passion of a dogmatist I decided to make a single handed attempt at remedying the situation.

This book is intended to be a tutorial for those who are not familiar with period firearms of the 1874–1881 era. The manuscript is most valuable when used in companion with a book about the Lincoln County War, such as my effort titled *Dead Right, The Lincoln County War,* or with one of the many reliable and detailed works of other noted Lincoln County War historians like Fred Nolan. His excellent books *The West of Billy the Kid* or *The Lincoln County War* are both highly recommended. When I first shouldered this undertaking I believed that this is one of those books "that needed to be written." A decade later I feel more strongly than ever. It should serve researchers, historians, and ardent enthusiasts well.

Acknowledgements

I was raised in a small rural town where doors were not locked and everyone knew everyone. As a youth I had access to firearms, and to competent training in their use. For that gift I am eternally grateful, and thank my father who made certain that I was enrolled in a Youth Program sponsored by the much now maligned National Rifle Association (NRA) of which I am a proud Life Member and avid supporter. It did not occur to me until many years later that not everyone had been so blessed. My interest in the history of the American West began at the age of thirteen, simultaneous with my passion for period firearms. I developed an avocation for collecting the trappings of cowboys, lawmen and outlaws. As with most undertakings, we generally need the help and support of others to bring our passion to a successful conclusion.

The list of those who have encouraged my study of the Lincoln County War, and my work on this particular book, is a long one. Needless to say the roster begins with my wife, who has tolerated my obsession with history, and collecting "junk," for decades. She has had a hand in rescuing me from countless bouts with chaos throughout this project and has endured my idiosyncratic behavior with little visible protest.

Others who top the list include my good friend James Owens of Hobbs, New Mexico. James's knowledge of, and passion for, the history of the Lincoln County War is impressive. His skills as a photographer, and collection of works in that venue is noteworthy. His life long, dogged pursuit of "all things Lincoln County" is a blessing to us all. Sharon Cunningham of Tennessee, a wonderful person and accomplished author ably combed through the original text in search of blunders. Gwendolyn Rogers formerly of the Lincoln State Monument at Lincoln, New Mexico generously encouraged and supported my work on the Lincoln County War. Her support predates that of practically everyone else, and came at precisely the instant when I needed it most. Historian, author and television personality Drew Gomber has been a good friend and confederate as well as a reliable resource.

Drew has always been there to help set me straight when folklore got in the way of history.

On the firearms side of the equation I have to recognize an old friend and mentor, Dick Capp of Evergreen, Colorado. Although Dick passed many years ago I am blessed to have many fond memories of him, whose signature greeting to all who were brave enough to carry an antique lever gun past his gun show table was, "how much will you take for that fine old Winchester?" I learned much from Dick, and from another old curmudgeon named Forest Reid McCandless. Much like ole "Dick" Capp in so many ways, Reid was known for his ability to take the parts from three Colt revolvers and manufacture four. Perhaps the best trader that ever stalked the corridors of a gun show. When it came to a bartering, Reid's was the grand master. His most noteworthy lines included, "there is bound to be some way we can trade on that old gun" and "Oh...there will have to be some difference...coming my way that is."

Sad to say that as the inevitable advance of old age begins to overtake me I have sold all of my precious antique guns and accoutrements. But although the guns are gone, the memory will long outlast them.

Ballad of a Trail-Weary
Trail-Herder

by
Reeves Axtell

The footsore doggies jam and crowd,
And poke along, and bawl and bleat,
Beneath a floatin', ashy cloud
That fogs their millin' horns and meat
And smudges up behind their feet
Till I'm half-choked and worse than blind—
Oh, gosh, the alkali I eat
A-ridin' here behind!
To swing the lead I'd shore be proud—
Sa-ay, wouldn't it be sweet
To get plumb free of this here shroud
That's all messed up with noise and heat?
Oh Misery shore grows complete
And weds itself to Fate unkind
When I'm the goat that has to beat
These drags along behind!
A week ago I would have vowed
That drivin' trail-herd was a treat;
I rode along a-singing loud
And plannin' how my gal I'd meet
In her ol' man's grape-arbor seat,
But now—the trail's just "mill and grind,"
And love songs shorely obsolete,
A-trailin' here behind.
Old horse, no fool has got me beat
For just plain softenin' of the mind—
But you kin hark to me repeat:
Trail-herdin's hell behind!

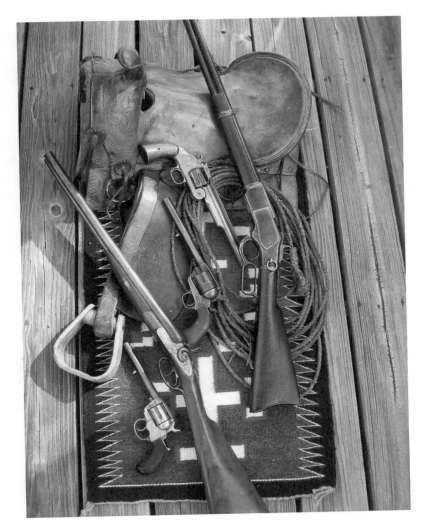

Period firearms

1

The Stage is Set

I was born not knowing
and have had only a little time
to change that here and there.
—Richard Feynman

Although the Lincoln County War is considered by most to have begun with the brutal murder of John Henry Tunstall on 18 February 1878, the build up to the conflict can reasonably be traced to the Horrell War, which occurred in 1873, and to John Chisum's Pecos War which took place not long thereafter. A case can be made that the roots of the conflict date to a time as early as the establishment of Fort Stanton in 1855, and the arrival of the first cattle drives from Texas in the early 1860s. Although some historians are divided on this point, most agree that the earliest cattle drives from Texas to New Mexico were headed up by either James Patterson or Robert Kelsey Wylie (or both). Apart from the fact that he was born in Ohio, reared in Illinois, and came to Texas and New Mexico in about 1859 or 1860, little is known about James Patterson prior to his involvement in the movement of stock to out of the Lone Star State. Robert Wylie worked for Patterson at Palestine, in Anderson County before the Civil War. Patterson is thought to have come to New Mexico near the onset of hostilities, and worked putting up hay and wood for one of the federal forts there.[1] During the war he was a beef contractor, operating at Fort Stanton and Fort Sumner, where he had a continued relationship with Wylie as well as John Chisum. Later, his presence is noted back in Texas where he was picking up herds and trailing them west to New Mexico.[2]

With the establishment of a military post at Fort Stanton there was suddenly a need for a local supply of goods and services. Enterprising citizens began to take advantage of the frequently corrupt military procurement process almost immediately, laboring to monopolize certain aspects of trade. The arrival of Texas cattlemen like James Patterson, Robert Kelsey Wylie, John Williamson, M.C. Smith and John Simpson Chisum with their seemingly inexhaustible supply of Texas beeves soon set up another conflict.[3] A rival local faction, under the control of Emil Fritz, Lawrence G. Murphy and James J. Dolan, resented the competition for the lucrative government contracts meted out by the military post. A deadly conflict was preordained. War in Lincoln was practically inevitable.

However, once underway, the Lincoln County War should have ended in the back yard of the Alexander A. McSween's house on 19 July 1878 with the killing of Mr. McSween. But...the wake of the bloody conflict continued until the subsequent killing of Henry McCarty (by then known as William Bonney or Billy the Kid) on 14 July 1881 at Fort Sumner, New Mexico. That considered, the period of time that is covered in this book begins with the Horrell War... in 1873, and ends with the death of Billy the Kid...in 1881.

Ethnic tensions had been festering in New Mexico Territory for a number of years. It was that which was underlying the difficulties that Ben Horrell, and before him John Hittson, encountered when they came into the country prior to the Pecos War. New Mexican historians might even cite an earlier conflict, the Pueblo Revolt of August 1680, as evidence of the fact that natives of the region resented intrusion.[4] As cited earlier, there was a deep seeded resentment on the part of persons of Mexican and Indian descent to the presence of any Anglo, especially Texans, in the territory. Much has been written about the Texan's rough treatment of Mexicans back home. Accurately focusing the lens of impartiality in this context is troublesome, and often steeped in ambiguity. Conclusive findings, skewed by perspective, are often thwarted. A balanced examination of Texas history will reveal ample instances. Such cases are far fewer than contemporary historians would wish one to believe. An ardent researcher, if so inclined, can uncover far more cases of cultural, ethnic and religious resentment by investigating the history of immigrant Italians, Irish, Chinese and Jews in America. But to what extent did this resentment come into play with regard to the Horrell clan?

The Horrell family hailed from near Lampasas, Texas. The father-son team of Benedict Horrell and son Sam left Kentucky around 1836 and located briefly at Hot Springs, Arkansas. From there they traveled to Texas; and in 1857 settled near Lucy Creek in the northeastern part of Lampasas County where they plied their trade as farmers and ranchers. Benedict "Ben" Horrell's first wife was Elizabeth Wells, whom he wed at Little Rock, Arkansas. His second wife was Sara Ann Wood. Altogether Ben had seven sons and one daughter: William C., John W., Samuel W., James "Mart" Martin, Thomas L., Benjamin F., C. Merritt, and daughter Sarah "Sally" Ann.

Said to have been "good neighbors who got along well with the locals" the family kept to themselves.[5] However, neighbor John Nichols later recalled that in a conversation with a local woman named Clements, Mrs. Horrell was quoted as saying, "...I raised my boys to be fighters." Mrs. Horrell might have been referring to the fact that her boys were, by then, already experienced Indian fighters. Indian depredations ravaged Lampasas County in the pre- and post-Civil War era, with raiding bands of Lipan, Apache and Comanche striking in small bands killing settlers and driving off their horses.[6]

Sympathetic to the cause of the Confederacy, the oldest Horrell brother, William C. "Bill" Horrell, joined the 18th Regiment of Texas Cavalry at the onset of the Civil War. He was never heard from after leaving home. It is believed he died of disease in 1862 during the war.[7]

In the wake of the Civil War, Texas was in turmoil. Reconstruction era politics favored punishing states that had been loyal to the Confederacy. The new government in Austin, run largely by former Federals called "carpetbaggers," did little to protect the settlers on the frontier. Indian depredations increased, as did general lawlessness, spawned in part by returning veterans who discovered they had lost everything while away. In light of the foregoing, Lampasas County had become an inhospitable place for the Horrells, so they began to round up their cattle in preparation for a move to California.[8]

While traveling through New Mexico Territory, they sold their herd at a good profit, but the trip proved to be a costly one for the family. On 7 January 1869, John W. Horrell was killed by a disgruntled cowhand named Early Hubbard in a dispute over wages.[9] A week later, the patriarch, "Old Sam," was killed when his party was ambushed by Apaches while traversing San Augustin Pass, about ten miles from Las Cruces.[10] The family's stay in New Mexico was brief. By 17 March 1869, the survivors had returned to Texas, passing by John Chisum's South Spring Ranch along the trail.[11]

Sympathetic locals in Lampasas, Texas regarded brothers Sam, Mart, Merritt, Tom, and Ben as "fun-loving cowboys."[12] However, that opinion of the Horrells was not shared by all. Late author and columnist Claude Douglas wrote that no family played a more prominent role in the lawlessness in Lampasas than the Horrells. They often shot up the town, and were counted among the group of outlaws who routinely rustled livestock and butchered other people's cattle. The local Lampasas newspaper, the *Dispatch*, remarked upon the playful habits of the indigenous ne'er-do-wells, describing how they had taken to firing their pistols at knotholes in walls of local building as they rode through town. The editor went on to lament that he had all but given up sitting behind glass windows since they were being shot out as fast as they could be replaced.[13]

On 14 January 1873, Lampasas County Sheriff Shadrack T. "Shade" Denson was shot and wounded during the noon recess of the district court.[14] Brothers George Washington "Wash" and Marcus "Mark" Short were involved, and one of the pair did the shooting.[15] When the district judge ordered the arrest of the Short brothers, Ben, Tom and Mart Horrell, along with their companion Patrick McGinty, drew their pistols on the arresting deputies and allowed the men to escape. A posse was hastily organized and headed out in pursuit. At the edge of town the lawmen were met by the Horrell boys and were briskly turned back when Ben Horrell told Tom Sparks, the leader, "no... you can't get them (Short brothers)."[16] The undaunted Sparks decided to have it out with the Horrells right then and there, but quickly backed off when Ben bailed from his horse and made ready for a fight. The posse returned to Lampasas with their collective tails between their legs.

In the face of increasing lawlessness, local authorities petitioned Governor Edmund J. Davis to send in the state police to help restore law and order.[17] As author C.L. Sonnichsen put it in *I'll Die Before I'll Run* the town was wide open and the saloonkeepers and gamblers had things their own way.[18] Police Captain Thomas G. Williams and seven state policemen were dispatched to Lampasas on 14 March 1873.[19] Although their attentions were to be directed at the Horrells, they were also charged with enforcing a new law that prohibited anyone from carrying a firearm in public. Almost immediately upon their arrival they saw a man named Bill Bowen sporting a revolver as he entered Jerry Scott's saloon. As cited in *Bad Blood*, Williams had no way of knowing that Bowen was a brother-in-law of the Horrells and that Jerry Scott's saloon was the favorite watering hole of the clan.

Most reports indicate that Captain Williams left three state policemen, including the lone black officer outside as he entered the saloon to arrest Bowen. He took police privates James Monroe Daniels, Wesley Cherry, and Andrew Melville with him as backup.[20] Another account lists four state policemen, not three, who remained outside the saloon that day.[21] A further and widely divergent version of the story alleges that Captain Williams disarmed and arrested Bowen before they entered the saloon.[22] Nonetheless, most agree that once Williams was inside the tavern he told Bowen "I see you are wearing a pistol...I arrest you."[23] Mart Horrell, described by neighbor John Nichols as "a round shouldered troublemaker," told Bowen he did not have to submit to the arrest. At that point Captain Williams is said to have drawn his pistol and fired, wounding Mart. In a slightly different account *The Union* newspaper indicated that while Williams and Bowen were grappling for the pistol Mart Horrell shot Williams.

Gunfire erupted as the ten to fifteen men in the confines of the small saloon pulled their guns. Although accounts of the battle differ widely, Williams was shot twice through the body and once in the head. Daniels was killed instantly from bullets to the head and body. Cherry made it outside before being killed. Melville was mortally wounded, having been shot through the left lung. Using what remaining strength he could muster Melville ran out of the saloon and across to the Huling Hotel. Tom Horrell was also wounded in the exchange. The remaining occupants of the saloon spilled out on the street where the shooting continued. The remaining state policemen (Henry Eddy, Ferdinand Marshal, Sam Wicks and W.W. Wren) promptly fled back to Austin. Policeman Andrew Melville died on 10 April 1873 of the wounds he received in the exchange.[24]

The following day at a hastily called inquest the names of the killers of Williams and his officers were identified as Tom, Merritt and Mart Horrell, Ben Turner, Joe Bolden, Allen Whitcraft, Jim Grizzell, Jerry Scott, Bill Bowen and Bill Gray. A posse was organized, and after making a five day scout through several counties Mart Horrell, Jerry Scott, James Grizzell and Allen Whitcraft were arrested and jailed at Georgetown, Texas. On the night of 2 May 1873 the remaining Horrell brothers, accompanied by a group of about thirty sympathizers, stormed the jail and freed them all.

Mark Short was arrested about three years later, but while in custody he was shot and killed by Sheriff Denson's son Samuel, who fled to Montana to evade the murder charge. He eventually returned to Texas about twenty years later and was acquitted.[25] Samuel Denson moved to California where he died on 10 July 1939. Former Sheriff Shadrack Denson died on 31 March 1892 of complications from the wound he had received in the shooting at Lampasas almost two decades earlier in 1873.

As a result of some difficulties that centered around allegations of disturbing the peace, which eventually led to the needless and completely avoidable killing of four Texas State Policemen on 14 March 1873, by late summer of that year Lampasas County, Texas was no longer a hospitable place for the Horrell bunch. They decided to head west to New Mexico. The clan had made that trip earlier, however. Considering the outcome it is surprising that they returned. On 7 January 1869 John W. Horrell had been bushwhacked and killed by a disgruntled cowhand named Early Hubbard in a dispute over wages at the completion of a cattle drive near Las Cruces.[26] The patriarch, "Old Sam," was killed on 14 January 1869 when his party was ambushed by Apache Indians while traversing San Augustin Pass about ten miles from Las Cruces.[27] Their stay in New Mexico was brief and costly. The remaining Horrell party had headed back to Texas by 27 March 1869.

Ready to decamp from their home in Texas, the family began to round up all of their cattle and make arrangements to sell a portion of the herd.[28] Some of the cattle were pre-sold to Cooksey & Clayton, and were delivered to Coleman County in route to New Mexico.[29] Although the entire extended family did not move en masse, the advanced contingent arrived in Lincoln County in the fall of 1873 with pockets bulging from the sale of their herd in Texas. The clan bought a ranch on the Rio Ruidoso, at the mouth of Eagle Creek, located not far from the present day village of Hondo. In *Bad Blood* the author states that according to local oral history the Horrells paid a man named Heiskell Jones forty dollars for a quit claim deed relinquishing his squatter's rights to the ranch. Others have claimed that Frank Regan, a partner of Jones, knew that the documents were worthless and that Lawrence G. Murphy & Co. had a lien on the property.[30] This was the same Lawrence G. Murphy who advanced the Horrells sufficient credit to begin their ranching operation in Lincoln.[31] Frank Coe, who later owned the ranch, believed they only "rented the place from Murphy and Dolan."[32] More Horrell kin, and twelve or fifteen common minded friends including Thomas Bowen, Jerry D. Scott and a man named Woods, began to settle in the area with their sizeable herd of Texas longhorn cattle.[33]

On 1 December 1873 Ben Horrell and former Lincoln County Sheriff Dave C. Warner, along with Jack "Texas Jack" Gylam, Zacharias Crompton and Jerry Scott rode into the town of Lincoln to pick up their mail.[34] Most historians have claimed that the group set about the town drinking and carousing. On further examination, that version of the day's events may be somewhat overstated.[35] Members of the predominantly Mexican population took issue with the revelry. Lincoln Constable Juan Martínez was summoned. He demanded that the men surrender their weapons. Grudgingly they complied, but it wasn't long before the bunch had rearmed and returned to their merriment. Martínez and a posse of Mexican Police Guard returned to confront Ben Horrell, David Warner and Jack Gylam. Martínez shot Warner, and Warner did the same for Martínez.[36] The Horrell bunch fled, but were chased down and murdered by the vengeful Mexicans, who shot Ben Horrell nine or ten times while he was on his knees begging for mercy.[37] Gylam is said to have been shot thirteen times.[38] One source claimed that he sustained three gunshot wounds before he surrendered. A pistol had been placed so

close to his body that his clothing had been burned by gunpowder. One shot had passed through his heart. His head was struck as if it had been done with a rock.[39]

The murder of Ben Horrell was not an isolated display of local cultural or ethnic strife. Major John Mason wrote from Fort Stanton in December 1873 that:

Another branch is the Texas Cowboys who bring in large herds of Texas Cattle, some to go north others remaining on the large tracts of fine grazing lands in this region. A bitter hatred exists on the part of the Mexicans against all Americans, who they think have no right to come in and occupy the lands which for so many years they have considered the exclusive heritage of the Mexicans, and you can very readily conceive that this hatred is reciprocated by the Texans. The Civil authorities at Lincoln are nearly all Mexicans, possibly one or two Americans, on(e) the sheriff (Ham Mills) whose wife is Mexican espouses the cause of the Mexicans—so long as these officially have a force of from fifteen to thirty well armed Mexicans they are very brave and full of bragadocia (braggadocio) and on all occasions when an outside party comes into their town on any business, this force is paraded and the parties disarmed.

Major Mason went on to write:

...angry feelings still exist and Mexicans still threatening. I learned that the Catholic priest advises them to surround and set fire to the Texans ranch houses and to kill all as they fled to the hills also that such an attempt was made last week also that one of the Mexican leaders a notorious scoundrel and cutthroat had gone to the town of Tularosa for reinforcements. This matter stood on Saturday night last where a Baile (dance) was given by the Mexicans in the courthouse at Placita (Lincoln) – Whilst engaged in dancing a volley was fired into the room by parties unknown and four Mexicans were killed and one or two wounded. Of course the Texans disowned this since their every effort has been made by the whites and better class of Mexicans to stop the feud and submit (?)

the question of civil tribunals. The Texans are now willing, as they always have been to agree to this but the Mexicans are not. The civil authorities absolutely refuse to act in the matter – but swear that they will go with their people and head the fight. Threats are made that no Americans shall live at the town or in the vicinity that all must leave.

Mason's assessment of the situation in Lincoln County, New Mexico circa 1873–1874 provides remarkable insight into what, practically to a man, historians have previously portrayed as a cultural and ethnic bias on the part of Texans against Mexicans. Such tradition is difficult to refute, but easy to edit out of one's account of the foregoing incident.

In the days following Ben Horrell's murder several failed attempts were made by the Lincoln mob to rout the Texans from their stronghold. Ultimately their raid on the Horrell ranch succeeded, but only after the brave and triumphant posse headed up by James Dolan discovered that the family had already departed Lincoln County, thus explaining why their barrage of gunfire had not been returned. This resulted in Dolan's dazzling victory. They captured of a vacant home.

While the truth lies somewhere in the middle, it is important to keep in mind that it is quite possible that notwithstanding the families' difficulties in Texas, the Horrells, along with their pets, rocking chair and four or five thousand head of cattle, may have come to New Mexico for the peaceful purpose of raising livestock and driving them to the lucrative markets that were not far distant. None-the-less, warrants had been issued for their arrest and it was time to break and run back to Texas. Their withdrawal to Texas was not without incident however, as they stole whatever they could find of value as they headed for more friendly haunts. During a stopover at Picacho, Edward "Little" Hart, a member of the group, murdered Deputy Sheriff Joseph Haskins. It is said that "Little" Hart's only reason for killing Haskins was that the deputy was married to a Mexican girl. Others killed by the Horrell bunch during February 1874 include Pedro Romero, Sevenano Apodaca, Juan Silva, Teferino Trujillo and Ramondo Apodaca.[40]

As many as eighty to one hundred people are said to have been killed during the Horrell War.[41] In

Ten Deadly Texans the authors make mention of the fact that years after the Horrell troubles in Lincoln County Frank Coe said that the killings of Ben Horrell and his group had been done on orders of Lawrence G. Murphy and James J. Dolan, by then referred to as "The House."[42] The authors also cite seizure of property belonging to the Horrells to pay debts owed Murphy as the underlying reason. Although Coe's proposition is entirely plausible, this writer is more inclined to assign responsibility for the fatal outcome of the Horrell clan's stay in New Mexico to the sharp ethnic divisions between Anglos and Mexicans prevalent at the time.

There was a sizeable population of Mexican immigrants who wielded a great deal of power in Lincoln County. In the end they gained the upper hand in the Horrell affair. At the same time, Murphy and Dolan's monopolistic control of trade and far reaching influence in Lincoln cannot be underestimated. But linking the Horrell conflict to the Lincoln County War, which would be fought to a mortal finish four years later, seems to be an oversimplification of the dynamics of the latter business, as well as a blanket condemnation of Lawrence G. Murphy and James J. Dolan. The Horrell family did not pose a threat to Murphy and Dolan in the same way that Alexander McSween and John Tunstall did by the spring of 1878. The rationale for the Horrell clan leaving New Mexico was far more complex than one author put it when he penned "... the boys grew tired of this rather monotonous fray..."[43]

The details of the Horrell incident in early 1874, do present a strong case that Murphy and Dolan had a hand in driving the group from the territory, however. Along with that pair the direct participation of James Dolan as well as the newly appointed sheriff, Murphy supporter, "Ham" Mills. Regardless of what else had been set in motion by the Horrell War, in the end Murphy gained absolute control of law enforcement in Lincoln after a community meeting on 27 January 1874. Soon afterwards, Juan Patron, respected leader of the local Mexican community, also mentioned that the pursuit of the Horrell clan had been instigated by the Murphy/Dolan faction, who benefited greatly from their hasty departure.[44]

So on balance, the Horrells found Texas to be a more hospitable place. The returning party arrived in Lampasas County during the last week of February

1874, claiming that "we fought them (New Mexicans) all the way to Fort Davis." The Horrells had no sooner hit Texas soil when they were met by a greeting party led by Lampasas County Sheriff Albertus Sweet. During the predictable skirmish that followed, Rufus Overstreet and Jerry Scott were captured, with the latter having been shot through the lung during the encounter. A wounded Merritt Horrell escaped, but was soon persuaded to surrender to authorities. In October of 1876 Tom, Mart, and Merritt Horrell were acquitted of the March 1873 killing of the four state policemen. The jury reached a verdict without leaving their seats. This might be considered as a further, sad testimonial to the extent of the degradation of law and order in Lampasas County, but on the other hand the state failed to produce any witnesses at the trial, and counsel determined that the state police had fired first.

Although the Horrells were now out of the way, affairs in Lincoln County were by no means calm. John Simpson Chisum was involved in a string of seemingly endless skirmishes along the Pecos River, with bouts of hostile gunfire taking place at various locations between his ranch at South Spring and the Loving Bend of the Pecos (below present day Carlsbad). From the onset, John Chisum had endeavored to gain total control of a fertile strip of rich grazing land along the river to pasture his thousands of head of cattle. The small local ranches resented Chisum's domination of the range and water resources which, prior to the Cattle King's arrival in 1867, had been open range, and used by all free grazers. Undaunted, the modest band of ranchers pushed back against Chisum's domination. A group of these stockmen generally referred to as "The Seven Rivers Gang" were led by rancher Hugh Beckwith.[45] In time John Chisum would have a full scale war on his hands along the Pecos.

Then as now, Texans take a dim view of cattle rustling. Wylie and Chisum were no exception. Wylie had a history of tracking down freebooters and seeing to it that they met justice. Soon, confrontations between the Texas free grazers and the Seven Rivers ranchers became commonplace. Making matters worse, trouble was brewing between Chisum and the duo, Murphy and Dolan. With local politics stacked against Wylie and Chisum, and the Murphy/Dolan faction manipulating local affairs behind the scene, their indirect involvement in the wholesale theft of Wylie and Chisum cattle went unchecked. Between the drain on the herd caused by the Seven Rivers crowd, and the emergence of the Murphy/Dolan mischief, losses mounted.

Wylie and Chisum objected. In retaliation, Warrant #125 was filed against Robert Wylie and his brothers for refusing to pay taxes. The taxes in question were due before 1 October 1874, and had to do with the herd that had become commingled with John Chisum's stock during the preceding winter of 1872–1873. Obviously the charges were patently false, but at the time the truth did not matter when it came to politics in Lincoln County. Witnesses to the delinquency were Juan Patron and Hamilton "Ham" Mills, both known tools of the Murphy/Dolan consortium. Having no legitimacy on its face, the warrant was eventually dismissed on 6 October 1875. Still, it was clear that the cattle kings were in for a fight.[46]

A confrontation was foreordained. The clash, known as *The Pecos War*, practically swallowed up the southeast corner of New Mexico Territory for two years. It was, in essence, a running gun battle between Chisum cowboys and the smaller cattlemen of Seven Rivers. Called by some *Chisum's Pecos War*, it is inexorably linked to the larger and far bloodier Lincoln County War. Although the conflict was largely spawned by Chisum, in all likelihood Robert Wylie and John Chisum's brother Pitser, took the leadership roles in many of the encounters during the affray because John was down with smallpox for much of the time.[47]

One of the first open clashes between the warring factions occurred in October 1876 at the Wiley Cow Camp, located about eighty miles below the Chisum Ranch at South Spring. A man named Thomas M. Yopp was in charge of the camp and became upset with two other Chisum cowboys while he was questioning the disappearance of some cattle.[48] Yopp drew his revolver and fired three shots at the first man, Thomas Benton "Buck" Powell. Powell seized his Winchester and shot Yopp in the mouth, taking him out of the fight temporarily. However, Yopp quickly rejoined the fight and resumed firing at Powell. Powell's Winchester jammed, so he grabbed Yopp's gun and shot him in the heart with it.[49]

On 10 March 1877 Chisum cowboy, gun hand,

and colleague from Trickham, Texas James M. Highsaw (Hysaw) rode into Wylie's cow camp on the Loving Bend of the Pecos River and confronted Dick Smith with what Highsaw believed was solid evidence of Smith's cattle rustling activities.[50,51,52] Highsaw was known to be "quick as lightning on the draw and cool under any circumstances." When Smith went for his gun the faster Highsaw beat him to the draw and shot him fatally. Two other known Seven Rivers cattle thieves, Charley Perry and Jake Owen, stood by and did nothing to help Smith. A gang of Seven Rivers ranchers including Bob and John Beckwith, Wallace Olinger, William Johnson, Andy Boyle, Milo Pierce, Lewis Paxton and Buck Powell (who had switched allegiances since the Wylie Cow Camp incident) pursued Highsaw and caught up with him at the Chisum ranch.[53] Insults, as well as a few rifle shots, were exchanged but ultimately the Seven Rivers men rode off without Highsaw.

In a later report about this incident to U.S. District Attorney Thomas B. Catron of Santa Fe by Seven Rivers rancher Andrew Boyle it was claimed that Dick Smith was "shot in the back five times with a Colt's improved .45 cal. six-shooter."[54] The two witnesses, William H. "Jake" Owen and Charles Perry, testified that "Smith was killed by revolver shots in the head, back and breasts fired by Highsaw."[55] Highsaw was indicted for the killing at the June 1877 term of court in Lincoln. When John Chisum failed to support his defense Highsaw fled to Texas.

According to one source, James M. Highsaw was related to Robert Wylie.[56] James Highsaw is believed to have born circa 1854, and probably in Texas. He was the son of William Highsaw of Alabama (some sources list his possible origin as South Carolina) and Lucinda Jordan (Jardon), also of Alabama. Highsaw's father worked for Thomas Samuel Wylie, Robert's brother, in the later 1850s in the area where Eastland and Erath Counties join. After the Civil War Thomas Wylie opened a general store at what was then known as Wylieville, now Hannibal. He was also the postmaster there.[57] Thomas Samuel, John Nixon and Henry Clay Wylie all settled in Erath County for a time. Prior to coming to Coke County in 1895, Thomas had 2,200 acres of land, 400 of which was under cultivation.[58] At Bronte, in Coke County, Thomas purchased 3,840 acres.[59]

As for Jake Owen, he went on to fight on the side of the Dolan Faction during the Lincoln County War.[60]

On 20 April 1877, Chisum and about thirty of his men struck out from the Wylie cow camp and surrounded the adobe home of the kingpin of the small Pecos ranchers, Hugh Beckwith. They cut off the Beckwith's water supply, threatened to starve them out, and demanded that they surrender and be brought to justice for cattle rustling. Instead of surrendering, the Beckwith crowd decided to shoot it out with the Chisum cowboys. That night two men, Charles Woltz and Buck Powell, proceeded to sneak past the Chisum cowboys and headed to Mesilla to try and obtain a warrant for the arrest of Wiley, Chisum and Highsaw for the murder of Dick Smith. On the 21st Wylie and Chisum sent in local ranchers Mr. and Mrs. Gray to try to convince Beckwith to send the women and children out to safety. The Beckwith clan refused to leave the house. On the 22nd Chisum's men began laying down a barrage of gunfire on the Beckwith place. They did so from a distance of over 500 yards, thus their pathetic fusillade fell upon the ranch house with no measurable effect. Chisum's cowboys refused to move closer, protesting that they had signed on to herd cows, not to get shot, for $30 a month. Frustrated, Chisum withdrew their men, restored the water flow and retreated to Wylie's cow camp on the Pecos.[61]

On 7 May 1877, Buck Powell and Charlie Woltz returned from Mesilla with warrants to be served on John Chisum and Robert Wylie. Andy Boyle, acting deputy sheriff at the time, assembled a posse consisting of Bob and John Beckwith, Wallace Olinger, William Johnson and Buck Powell. They went out to the Wylie camp and found John Chisum. He was gravely ill with smallpox. Afterwards they rode to the Chisum ranch where they found Wylie. Apart from the warrants they had to serve, the group contended that Chisum owed them wages in arrears. Wylie promised that checks would be issued for all sums due.[62] Wylie ultimately produced the appropriate remuneration, and all of the men were paid.[63]

On 20 June 1877, an indictment was obtained in Mesilla against Wylie, Chisum, Highsaw and Thad Hendricks for theft of livestock from the Beckwith ranch. In total the document detailed seventeen horses valued at $500 each, ten mules valued at $500 each and seventeen mares at $500. Later in 1877 this and all other warrants against Wylie and Chisum were either dropped or stricken from the docket.

Thus by the end of 1877 the Pecos War had drawn to a close, but hard feeling remained on the part of the Seven Rivers ranchers that would carry over into the next, and vastly more deadly conflict.

Former military officer Lawrence G. Murphy had formed a partnership with Lieutenant Colonel Emil Fritz at Fort Stanton in 1868. Murphy had been an officer in the army, and had been promoted to the rank of major for his meritorious service in the Navajo Wars. Fritz had been commander of the First Regiment, California Cavalry, and was post commander of Fort Stanton by November 1865.[64]

Murphy established a store and brewery on the Mescalero Indian Reservation at the eastern edge of Fort Stanton. Fritz also owned a ranch located about eight miles below Lincoln along the Rio Bonito. In the summer of 1870 the post at Fort Stanton was enlarged, and L.G. Murphy and Company became a privately owned island in the midst of government property. The partners made the most of this opportunity. In effect, they became both sellers of provisions to the military in the field and Indian traders. Their store and brewery were the only such establishments on the property. The Bureau of Indian Affairs never designated Murphy's business as an Indian trader, but he continued to operate as if it had and enjoyed the benefits of being a monopoly. Murphy also managed to get elected as Probate Judge of Lincoln County, expanding his local influence and enabling him to wield a considerable amount of power. Eventually Murphy developed a strong and seemingly unbreakable monopoly on most commercial transactions at Fort Stanton. His enterprise secured contracts from the Army to supply grain and hay to the fort. This gave them leverage and control over the local farmers and ranchers who were forced to sell to Murphy, as there was no other local market. They also had the contracts for the supply of beef, which was purchased on the hoof and at the best price available. Fritz and Murphy soon included a young Irishman named James Joseph Dolan in their business.[65] Dolan had gone to work for Fritz and Murphy as a clerk after

he was discharged from the United States Infantry in 1869 and over time played a more significant role in their affairs. The L.G. Murphy Company prospered, but soon turned controlling and arrogant. The local farmers had little choice but to sell their produce to the company and to purchase supplies from them. Murphy's company set prices for both sale and purchase. Conflict soon arose as others including John Simpson Chisum and the newly arrived Englishman John Henry Tunstall sought to compete for the lucrative business at Fort Stanton. Lawyer Alexander McSween, who had previously been in the employ of L.G. Murphy, aided Tunstall in this endeavor.

Armed with poorly conceived plans engineered largely by McSween the pair labored to form their own ring, and to monopolize the fort's business themselves. Hostilities between the two rival factions erupted into open warfare when on 18 February 1878 members sympathetic to the Murphy/Dolan faction murdered John Tunstall.

Friends and supporters of Tunstall and McSween rallied to avenge the despicable assassination of John Tunstall. Young William Bonney, soon to be known as Billy the Kid, had been befriended by Tunstall, was inspired by this cause. Bonney would emerge as the unlikely hero, and be a significant player in the outcome of the upcoming confrontations. The small mountain community of Lincoln was now irreconcilably divided, and would endure five months of continuous conflict as supporters of Tunstall and McSween battled the Murphy/Dolan faction.

Ambushes, shoot outs and running gun battles punctuated the coming months, all culminating with the bloody five day siege at the home of Alexander McSween in July 1878. Billy the Kid would emerge from the fire, smoke and ashes of the inferno and begin a three year journey playing hero and villain simultaneously, culminating with his death at the hand of Sheriff Pat Garret in Fort Sumner, New Mexico in July 1881.[66]

The full, historically accurate account of the Lincoln County War is contained in this author's book *Dead Right, The Lincoln County War*. The purpose of this book covers the firearms that were available between 1873 and 1881, and many of the guns that were known to have been used by the participants.

From period photographs we are able to

determine that participants in the Lincoln County War were, for the most part, armed with the best and latest weaponry available. Although Lincoln may seem to be a long way from the population centers of the country at the time, the supply lines for goods had already crisscrossed the whole of the west. Railroads provided service to major distribution centers like St. Louis. From there links reached to within miles of Santa Fe, with service terminating at nearby Lamy. From Lamy goods traveled by wagon to the stores in Lincoln such as those operated by L. J. Murphy and Company and John Henry Tunstall.

But the firearms, and not the conflicts, are the focus of this book. By 1873 there was a wholesale conversion underway from muzzle loading percussion firearms to the more modern metallic cartridge guns. In addition, the single shot weapons were being replaced by more sophisticated repeating firearms. Both evolutionary steps were game changers as far as armed conflict is concerned.

Lincoln County Courthouse.

2

The Cartridge Firearms

Death can sneak up on you like a silent kitten,
surprising you with its touch
and you have a right to act surprised.
Other times death stomps in the front door,
unwanted and unannounced,
and makes its noisy way to your seat on the sofa
—Hugh Elliott

It has been said that the advent of rifling in the gun barrels of weapons, coupled with the use of the newly designed bullet called the Minie Ball, were the two major factors behind the enormous casualties that were witnessed during the Civil War.[67] The invention of the metallic cartridge proved to be the vehicle by which rapid fire and reloading could be accomplished, thus upping the tally of casualties in an armed conflict. These two factors contributed greatly to the changing face of warfare. It is significant that the conversion from muzzle loading firearms to metallic cartridge firearms was unfolding at the time of the Lincoln County War.

The move to metallic cartridge firearms began with the invention of fulminate of mercury by a British chemist named Howard. Howard's invention made it possible for the Reverend Alexander Forsyth of Belhelvie, Aberdeenshire, Scotland to invent the modern percussion primer that would profoundly change modern firearms. For those unfamiliar with the story, Reverend Forsyth, who was an avid hunter, observed that waterfowl were started by the flash and puff of smoke emitted from the frizzen pan of his flint-lock shotgun. The visible evidence of the weapon's discharge gave the birds sufficient warning to begin to take flight and thereby escape the arrival of the lead shot that followed the ignition of the gunpowder charge. The invention of a fulminate primed firing mechanism eliminated the puff of smoke, and greatly shortened the interval between the time the trigger

was pulled and the time the powder was ignited, driving the shot from the muzzle of the firearm.[68] Fulminate primed guns were also less likely to misfire than were their flintlock predecessors. The primer itself was made by placing a measured amount of fulminate of mercury into a small cup shaped piece of copper about the diameter of a pea. The primer was then placed over a nipple located at the breach of the firearm. The hole through the nipple led to the base of the barrel of the weapon. When the trigger was pulled and the hammer of the gun struck the nipple containing the primer and sent a flash of ignited fulminate of mercury down through the hole in the nipple which ignited the gunpowder charge at the base of the barrel. The exploding powder created pressure, thereby propelling the bullet out towards the open end of the barrel. In 1812 French inventor Jean Samuel Pauly filed his patent for a self-contained, self primed, center fire metallic cartridge.[69]

There are two types of self primed cartridges—rimfire and centerfire. In the instance of the rimfire cartridge the fulminate of mercury primer is placed in the base of a cylindrical shaped brass cartridge that has an extremely thin bottom (when compared to the center fire cartridge). Once primed, the gunpowder is inserted into the cartridge, followed by the bullet. The bullet is then lightly crimped in place to hold it securely. The rimfire cartridge is then inserted into the firing chamber of the weapon and the breach closed. The hammer of the weapon is then cocked, and when the trigger is pulled it releases the hammer which strikes the rim or base of the cartridge. The impact ignites the primer material, which in turn sets off the gunpowder causing an explosion. The powder explosion creates pressure, allowing the bullet to escape in the only direction possible, down the barrel of the weapon. In the case of the rimfire cartridge the hammer need not strike the base of the cartridge in the center. Anywhere on the base is sufficient. The centerfire cartridge functions in a similar manner. In essence the aforementioned primer containing the fulminate of mercury is installed in a pocket or hole at the base of the cylindrically shaped brass cartridge. The cartridge base, in this case, is much thicker. The powder is placed in the cartridge, followed by the bullet, which again is lightly crimped in place. In the case of the center fire cartridge the tip of the hammer, or firing pin, must strike the primer dead center in order to hit the primer and ignite it. This required a different shaped hammer, or a separate firing pin mechanism. Second, and perhaps more significant, once fired the exhausted center fire cartridges are reusable.

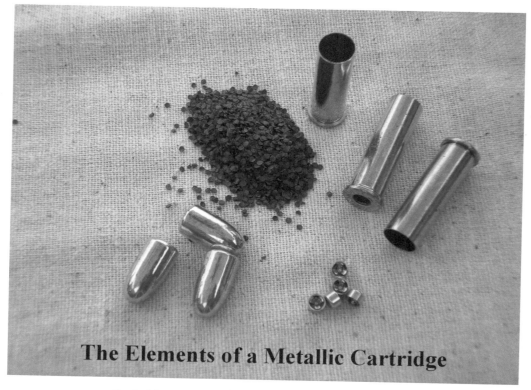

The Elements of a Metallic Cartridge

Cartridge case, primer, powder and projectile.

To reuse the spent cartridge case all one needed do was remove the expended primer and install a new one, reload the gunpowder, insert the bullet and crimp it in place. For the more technically inclined reader there are some issues with regard to trimming the case length and resizing the diameter that come into play with modern, high pressure smokeless cartridges. However, the center-fire cartridge cases in use during the 1870–1880s were generally reloaded "as is" by all but the most zealous shooters. Generally speaking, it was not until Paul Vieille invented smokeless gunpowder in 1884, and refined its formulation in 1886, that problems such as the pressure of the powder explosion against the brass cartridge causing its elongation and deformation became a problem and required these additional steps in the reloading of centerfire cartridges.

The early metallic cartridge firearms were almost all single shot weapons. The breech of the gun could be opened with some form of lever or mechanism allowing the cartridges to be inserted one at a time. In 1836 Samuel Colt invented the first revolving cylinder handgun called the Paterson Model.[70] The Paterson Colt was a muzzle loading weapon, and was sold in 2½ to 12 inch barrel lengths. The majority of the Paterson Colts that were produced had a 7½ or 9 inch barrel length. Bore diameter, or caliber, came in a wide variety of choices including .28, .31, .34, and .36 caliber. In 1855

Smith & Wesson's licensed Rollin White's 1854 patent for a cartridge revolver with the cylinder bored through from end to end, which allowed the cartridge to be inserted from the rear. This, as they say, changed everything.

Cartridges from .32 caliber rimfire to 50/110 Express.

A number of manufacturers began to introduce small caliber revolvers with five or six cylinders almost immediately. Some had cylinders that were removed by loosening a center pin. Some had frames that opened to facilitate loading. Others had a plethora of clever mechanisms. A person could now load and fire multiple time from a weapon without having to stop and reload after each shot. Reloading was made vastly simpler with the use of the self contained metallic cartridge. Although the early muzzle loading revolving pistols made by Colt and others did have five or six chambers, the gunpowder would often become wet causing the weapon to misfire. These revolvers were prone to crossfire, which is a rather frightening event that occurs when one chamber of the pistol is fired and a spark from the ignition leaps to the next chamber and ignites it (or to several other chambers). Keep in mind that only one chamber of the revolver is in line with the barrel, so when this simultaneous ignition takes place the lead ball that is fired from the other chamber (or chambers) strikes the frame of the revolver. In this instance the gun often explodes in the shooter's hand, with fragments of lead, and the pistol, flying in all directions. Results could be fatal, and often were.

Loading a percussion revolver required the user to pretty much stop whatever they were doing and charge each cylinder individually. The shooter had to introduce a measured amount of gunpowder then insert a lead ball into each cylinder one at a time. Next one drove the lead ball home with a ramrod or similar device. Finally one had to re-prime each of the five or six nipples with a new primer. This process took even the accomplished user more than a minute to complete, and in many cases two minutes or more depending on the individual's dexterity. With the advent of the metallic cartridge the process of reloading a revolving pistol could be accomplished swiftly, even while galloping along on horseback.

The next major betterment in firearm design came with Benjamin Tyler Henry's improvement in the late 1850s.[71] His design completely prevented gas leakage from the back, or breach of the firearm. With Henry's improvement the brass casing would expand on ignition and seal the chamber. This design was a betterment over Lewis Jennings' magazine fed lever action rifle. Soon after a machinist working in Hartford, Connecticut for the firearms maker Christian Sharps named Christopher Spencer invented the Spencer Repeating Rifle. The Spencer was the most advanced infantry weapon in the world at the time and was patented in 1860. One can see from the photo that a metallic center fire cartridge is comprised of several components, including a cartridge case which is usually made of brass or brass alloy, a projectile or bullet that is made of lead, gunpowder and a primer. During the manufacture of a center-fire cartridge the primer is inserted into the base of the metallic cartridge case. Next the powder is measured and loaded, the bullet is inserted and crimped into the cartridge case thereby completing the assembly. Although these cartridges were manufactured, boxed, and available through local stores such as L.J. Murphy and Company, cowboys and frontiersmen were able to save their expended brass cartridge cases and reload the cartridges themselves. A small set of tools and dies no larger than a pair of pliers was available and was often carried in saddlebags. A single or multiple cavity mold that looked like a small pair of pliers was used to form the lead bullet. One can imagine the Regulators, camped somewhere along the Rio Ruidoso, cleaning their weapons and reloading their cartridges by the dim light of a campfire.

.44 cal. Henry Rimfire.

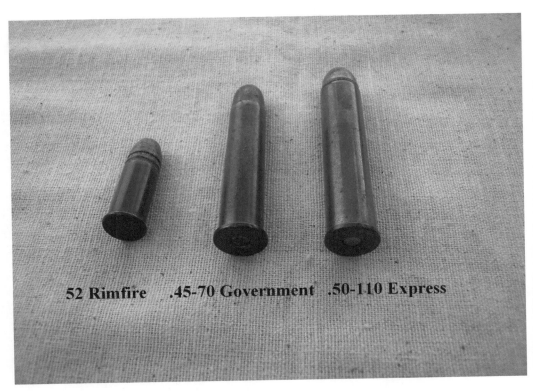

52 Cal Rimfire to 50/110 Express.

By 1873 Colt was already manufacturing a large frame open top revolver called the Model of 1872.[72] This gun was chambered for the .44 Caliber rimfire metallic cartridge. Colt had also begun to introduce their "strap pistol" called the Model "P." The Model "P," often called the Peacemaker, was officially identified by Colt as the Colt Single Action Army Model of 1873. Colt had been converting many of their older percussion models, like the Army Model of 1860 and Navy Model of 1851, to use the newer metallic cartridge. Smith & Wesson had long since been producing a cartridge firearm, starting with the Lever Action Magazine Pistol for which a patent was received and production began as early as 1854. The "Big Iron" Smith & Wesson guns were not produced until about 1870, starting with the American Model in .44 Caliber American, S&W and Russian and followed by the Second Model American and the famed Schofield, which was produced in caliber .45 Schofield. [73]

As far as long arms were concerned, every self respecting gun hand of the old west was armed with a Winchester. The origins of the quintessential Winchester actually predated the legendary Henry rifle, which was first offered for sale on 8 August 1854. The design of the Henry was improved upon, and the gun was eventually replaced by the Winchester Model 1866, which hit the market on 22 May 1866. The Model 1866 was simply called "The Winchester", since no other models or versions had yet been introduced by Oliver Winchester. The Model 1866 was chambered in the .44 Henry rimfire. Although the .44 Henry rimfire was huge improvement over the paper cartridges of the day it was still a woefully inadequate round for use in a long arm. By 1873 Oliver Winchester had improved on his long gun design and introduced the Model of 1873. The 1873, or "73" as it was called, was first offered in the .44-40

W.C.F. cartridge. The term .44-40 W.C.F. means a .44 caliber projectile propelled by 40 grains of black powder. The designation W.C.F. means "Winchester Center Fire." This nomenclature identified the piece of ammunition. The new cartridge proved to be an excellent one, and is still widely used today. The .44-40 was later adopted by Colt in their revolvers as early as 1878 and thus made an excellent companion piece to the Winchester rifle in the same caliber enabling the user to carry one cartridge for either firearm.

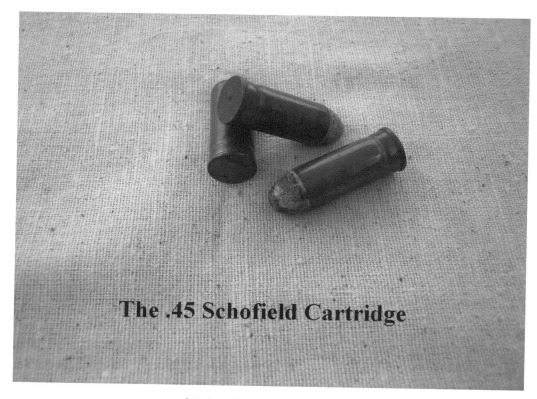

.45 Cal. Schofield Cartridge

There were numerous other cartridge firearms produced between 1873 and 1881, made by manufacturers such as Marlin, Remington, Merwin Hulbert, Sharps, Spencer, and Whitney Kennedy. There were also a seemingly infinite number of producers of shotguns during this same time period, with many excellent examples imported from Belgium and England.

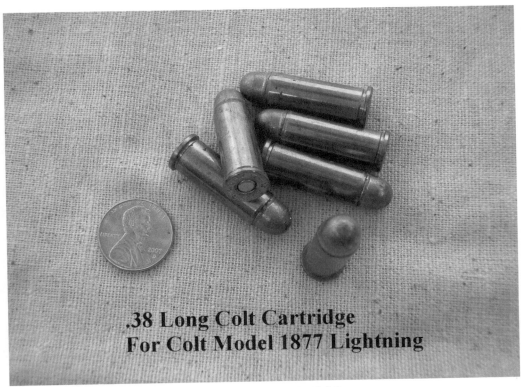

**.38 Long Colt Cartridge
For Colt Model 1877 Lightning**

.38 Cal Long Colt Cartridge

**.41 Long Colt Caliber
For Colt Model 1877 Thunderer**

.41 Cal. Long Colt Cartridge

3

The Legendary Colt

God created man.
Sam Colt made them all equal.

There is no better place to begin a discussion about revolvers than with the legendary Colt. Although well worn and perhaps a little trite, no discussion of the Colt firearm would be complete without the above quote. Although it sounds like a lofty claim in the early days of the American West it was largely accurate.

Sam Colt was born 19 July 1814 in Hartford, Connecticut. As a lad he went to sea as a cabin boy and through observation of a ships wheel in operation it is said that he envisioned the mechanism for a revolving firearm. Colt began manufacturing guns in his New Jersey factory in 1836. Early models during the period 1838 to 1840 included the famed Paterson model, first used by Texas Rangers during their many battles with Indians on the Texas frontier. He also produced a line of revolving cartridge rifles and carbines. Production was limited, and the guns became obsolete once the lever action rifles made by Oliver Winchester hit the market. By 1847 Sam Colt's business was on a better financial footing. In that year the famed Walker Colt was introduced. It was an enormous firearm that weighed in at four pounds, eight ounces and had a barrel length of sixteen inches. The Walker model fired six .44 caliber round lead balls and were manufactured for only a brief period of time in 1847. The gun was named after Captain Samuel Hamilton Walker, a renowned hero who had fought in the Texas-Mexico wars.[74] While in Washington D.C. Walker approached Samuel Colt and provided his input regarding an improved design revolver that would better suit the Texas Rangers and the U.S. Dragoons. The new weapon, based on the earlier Paterson model, featured many improvements. The new gun turned out to be so massive that Colt was reported to have commented, " it would take a Texan to shoot it."[75] In 1847 Walker commented about the improved Colt pistol, saying that it was " as effective as a common rifle at 100 yards and superior to a musket even at 200."

An array of various Colt pistols followed the Walker model. The list includes the Dragoon, the Model 1849 Pocket, the Model 1851 Navy, 1855 Side Hammer, the 1860 Army and 1862 Police. All of these were muzzle loading, percussion, revolving firearms. It is quite doubtful that any of them were widely used in the Lincoln County War since the conversion to cartridge firearms was well underway by that time.

Sam Colt did not live to see the full impact of his creation. He died on 10 January 1862, one year after the start of the Civil War. His six-guns accompanied soldiers wearing both blue and gray through the many battles of the War Between the States, and afterwards as pioneers made their way across the western frontier.

By 1873 Colt's company was making an all out effort to compete with Smith & Wesson. Smith & Wesson gained an advantage over Colt when they introduced their large frame, big caliber cartridge revolver in 1870. The Smith & Wesson pistol used the .44 caliber rimfire metallic cartridge that Colt had chambered for its 1860 Army Richards, Richards-Mason, and Thuer conversions. Colt had just begun to introduce their "strap pistol", known as the Colt Single Action Army Model of 1873 Model "P," generally referred to as the "Peacemaker."

The legendary Peacemaker was the tool of the cowboy, lawman and outlaw alike. When the Horrell War began in 1873 Colt had just begun to produce this new and innovative firearm, and had made only 3,501 of them the first year. Most of that year's production went to the U.S. Army, so it stands to reason that the six shooters used in the early days of the Horrell War were either Smith & Wesson American models or early Colt cartridge conversions like the 1st Model Richards.

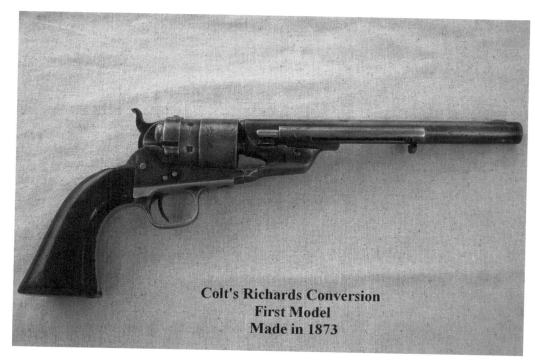

Colt's Richards Conversion
First Model
Made in 1873

Richard's Conversion of Colt Model 1860 Army

Richard's Conversion of Colt Model 1860 Army

The Model of 1873 caught on fast. It was first introduced for testing in .44 caliber rimfire, but that caliber selection was quickly changed to the now famous .45 Long Colt, colloquially referred to as the *Colt 45*. The .45 Colt is obviously a superb caliber, and it has survived for more than one hundred and thirty five years and is still widely used today.

The .45 Long Colt was the only production caliber offered in the Model 1873 until 1878. Before long Colt began to offer the gun in the popular .44-40 W.C.F. caliber that had been introduced by Winchester. The only barrel length available until the middle of 1875 was the 7½ inch. In 1875 the 5½ inch barrel was introduced, followed by the 4¾ inch in 1879. A vast number of the 7½ inch barrel guns were produced, and many have had their barrels shortened over the years to an array of odd lengths ranging from 7½ inch and 4½ inch. As a practical matter, one can not shorten the barrel of a Model 1873 further than about 4½ inches and still retain the function of the ejector rod, which is mounted in a housing along side the barrel and is used to eject the spent cartridges from the cylinder. Colt did, however, introduce a line of Model 1873 revolvers referred to as "Sheriff Models" that had shorter barrel lengths.

Factory Engraved Colt Model 1873

They were first introduced in 1878 (although none have been authenticated from that year). Those guns did not have an ejector rod assembly, and came in barrel lengths as short as about 2½ inches. Only one-piece wood grips were offered on Model 1873s until 1882 (with the exception of the occasional ivory or mother of pearl option). If one sees a gun in a museum somewhere that is represented as being from the period of the Lincoln County War that does not have one piece wood grips one may assume that it has either been altered or is a fraud.

When the Lincoln County War began any participant who had a Colt Model 1873 Single Action Revolver would have had a .45 Long Colt caliber model with a 7½ or 5½ inch barrel and one piece wood grips. This includes the combatants, on both sides, who participated in the running gun battle and capture of Buck Morton, the killing of Sheriff Brady, the shootout at Blazer's Mill, and the ambush at the Fritz Ranch. It's important to note that in all likelihood they did not all carry Colt revolvers. Many of them were armed with a Smith & Wesson, Merwin Hulbert, or some other less costly brand of firearm.

Colt Model 1873 Single Action Army 7½" Barrel

While James Dolan was busy planning to outmaneuver John Tunstall and Alexander McSween, Colt was in the process of introducing their first double action revolver. With a single action revolver one must pull back the hammer and cock the gun, bringing the hammer to the full cock position (known as "battery") before the trigger can be pulled and the weapon fired. This process must be repeated each time the user shoots the weapon. There is, of course, the method of "fanning" the single action revolver. That process basically involves holding the trigger in the full back position and rapidly fanning the hammer with the opposite hand, thereby firing the weapon and advancing the cylinder to the next chamber each time. This process results in discharging all six shots in rapid succession. Fanning generally results in the user spraying bullets in every direction and hitting nothing. Few, if any, real old west outlaws or lawmen actually employed this method of firing a gun. For the most part Hollywood invented "fanning" in the 1920s for your viewing enjoyment.

The double action revolver, or "self cocker" as it was called, would automatically advance the cylinder to the next chamber each time the trigger was pulled. That eliminated the need to manually cock the hammer between bouts with pulling the trigger. The user could pull the trigger six times, in rapid succession, and discharge all six rounds with some degree of accuracy. The first such model introduced by Colt was the Model of 1877, often incorrectly called the "Lightning."

Colt Model 1877

Colt Model 1877

The model of 1877 was produced in three calibers, .41 Colt which was called the Thunderer, the .38 Colt which was called the Lightning, and the .32 Colt which was called the Rainmaker. The guns were offered in nickel or blue finish and came with barrel lengths that ranged from as short as two inch to a few rare specimens that are said to be 12 and 14 inches. The most common barrel length was 4½ inch. The gun had a classic looking "birds head" shaped grip, which was easier for users with smaller hands to grasp firmly. The trendy Model 1877 was notoriously unreliable. If you have ever disassembled one you will find them to be filled with tiny, delicate parts that do not stand up to hard use. As a result, the guns popularity rapidly faded. They were best used as a pocket or purse gun, back up gun, a storekeeper's companion, or a gun to be kept in a dresser drawer for home protection. The Model 1877 was discontinued and replaced with a more reliable design in 1909 after 166,849 had been produced. By the time the Lincoln County War began it is highly unlikely that more than a handful of these guns could have reached Lincoln, perhaps none. Only 3,000 were made during the first year of manufacture.

Some 1877s had reached Lincoln County by the time Billy the Kid was killed on 14 July 1881. All of them would have had checkered one-piece rosewood grips. Guns made after 1882 had hard rubber, or gutta percha grips. All would have had the caliber marking on the side of the barrel etched with acid, reading either *Colt D. A. .38* or *Colt D. A. .41*. Later guns were marked with a die that struck an impression in the side of the barrel. It would not be until 1890 that the die marking method became standard.

Early Model Colt 1877 with Etched Panel Caliber Identification and One Piece Grips.

Extremely Rare Model 1877 Colt with 2" Barrel.

There were other problems with the Colt Model 1877 besides the unreliable double action mechanism. The caliber selections were woefully inadequate. The largest caliber offered in the Model 1877 was the .41 Colt, but the .38 Colt was the most popular based on sales. The .41 Colt did have some stopping power, but most users wanted larger bore weapons. Calibers like the .45 Colt or .44-40 W.C.F. offered better performance, range and stopping power. By comparison, the effective range of a handgun of this period was about thirty five to fifty yards, although most pistol shots in the old west were at much closer range. A .38 Short Colt bullet fired from a Colt Model 1877 revolver leaves the barrel at only 700 feet per second in velocity and packs a puny 130 foot pounds of energy at fifty yards. The .45 Long Colt projectile leaves the barrel at nearly 1,000 feet per second and retains about 400 foot pounds of energy at fifty yards. Some report that eighty five foot pounds of energy is sufficient to inflict a fatal injury to a human. Experiments on a material called ballistic jelly, which simulates a human body, have shown that a .38 caliber revolver bullet will perforate the skin and lodge in the underlying tissue at about 200 feet per second. It is more widely believed that the amount of energy required to effectively stop an average size man is closer to 400 foot pound. One can see from the arithmetic that the .38 Colt was not adequate to get the job done at anything other than very close range.

Example of "Etched Panel"
Caliber Identification
On Colt Revolvers

Thus, as cited earlier, in response to the need for more powerful calibers Colt introduced the larger Model of 1878 Double Action. The 1878 is a large frame gun, but retained the classic "birds head" type grip found on the Model 1877. Like the Single Action 1873 model, the 1878 was offered in a variety of calibers, barrel lengths, and grip choices. Early models had checkered wood grips like the 1877, but production was converted to hard rubber almost immediately. Unfortunately the Model of 1878 had many of the same problems as the 1877. It too was often unreliable due to its delicate and complicated mechanism. Only 51,210 Model 1878s were produced before production ceased in 1905. There were only been 4,000 of these guns manufactured by the start of 1881. Some found their way to the American West, and were initially a very popular firearm. One of Colt's largest distributors, and in all likelihood John Tunstall's supplier for his Lincoln store, was Simmons Hardware in St. Louis. Simmons moved into their new facility in 1879, and placed their first order for Colt 1878 model that same year. Marshal D.P. Upham of Fort Smith, Arkansas ordered four Model 1878s with 7½ inch barrels in .45 Colt caliber.[76] J.P. Lower of Denver ordered four Model 1878s in 1879, all with checkered ivory grips. In 1880 a few more of these Colt 1878s were shipped to the west. Distributors as close to Lincoln as Walter Tipps in Austin, Texas purchased several of them. Only about 500 were shipped the entire year of 1879, and that included a large number for export. George Maledon, the hangman for legendary Judge Isaac Parker, favored the Colt 1878 model and carried two of them.[77] Buffalo Bill Cody and Pawnee Bill ordered Model 1878s in 1888.[78] It is possible that some participants in the post Lincoln County War pursuit of Billy the Kid might have carried a Model 1878 revolver, but there were still comparatively few in circulation.

Last but not least is the line of Colt derringers. Derringers are basically pocket guns, and are useful as a "last line of defense." Colt made three versions in the large, .41 caliber size. Total production of all three designs was about 45,000, with manufacturing dates between 1870 and 1912. Perhaps as many as four to five thousand were in circulation by the time of the Lincoln County War.

That sums up the variety of Colt firearms that were available between 1874 and 1881, with the exception of the Burgess. The Colt Burgess lever action rifle and carbine were made from 1883 to 1885. This lever gun was part of Colt's plan to provide a well-rounded complement of firearms to the shooting public. Produced in caliber .44-40 W.C.W., in both carbine and rifle form, just a little over 6,000 were manufactured. At about the same time that Colt tooled up to produce the Burgess lever gun Winchester set out to manufacture a line of revolvers to compete with Colt. The two companies met and discussed the foolishness of competing with each other, engineering an agreement whereby Colt would drop the Burgess line and Winchester would not produce handguns. Although such an arrangement would violate present day antitrust laws it proved to be an effective covenant for the two firearms giants.

Colt Model 1878 Revolver with 7½" Barrel.

4

The Smith & Wesson

At the risk of exaggeration, one could say that Sam Colt received all the praise and Smith & Wesson did all the work. Thanks to Hollywood, and John Wayne, the legendary Colt revolver was thought by many of my generation to have been the only handgun used in the old west. In Plymouth, Michigan the Daisy Air Rifle Company produced thousands of BB guns that emulated the Colt peacemaker. Inexpensive, pot metal copies of the weapon were produced as cap guns, and adorned the belts of most young boys of the 1940s and 50s. Perhaps not until the introduction of the .44 Magnum revolver made famous by Clint Eastwood's movie *Dirty Harry* did anyone paid much attention to Smith & Wesson. If one is familiar with firearms, and old west history, one may believe as the author does that the Smith & Wesson revolvers of the late 1800s were quite possibly the finest, easiest loading and shooting, most reliable handgun ever produced. Although conceivably a boastful assertion, the Smith & Wesson pistol is, without question an excellent firearm.

Of the "Big Iron" Smith & Wesson revolvers the first to gain popularity was the First Model American. The American is a large pistol, weighing a hefty 41 ounces. It has an 8 inch barrel and fires the .44 S&W caliber cartridge. The American is a six shot, top break weapon. The term top break means that the locking mechanism, when released, enables the user to tilt the barrel forward from the hinge point on the frame in front of, and below, the cylinder. Once opened the operator has full access to all six cylinders for loading. The mechanism is also designed to extract and eject all six cartridges once they have been fired which further aided and accelerated the process of reloading. This feature alone made the gun vastly superior to the Colt in the opinion of many. The First Model American was only made for a brief time. Production totaled about 8,000, with manufacturing dates between 1870 and 1872. "Texas Jack" Omohundro is on the list of noted Old West personalities who favored this particular weapon was, and is claimed to have owned serial number 2,008.[79]

The First Model American was followed by the improved version, the Second Model American. The Second Model was offered in .44 S&W caliber, along with the .44 Henry Rimfire, which was the same cartridge used in the Winchester rifle of the day (the Model 1866). This new model came in several choices of barrel length, including 5, 5½, 6, 6¼, 6½, 7 and 8 inch, and came with a blue or nickel finish.

Smith & Wesson produced 20,735 of these revolvers between 1872 and 1874. The gun was very popular in the west. Wyatt Earp is said to have carried serial number 20,029 to the shootout at the OK Corral. On the opposite side of the law, Cole Younger favored the Second Model American. It has been claimed that Watonwan County Minnesota Sheriff Glispin and posseman George Adam Eagle took serial number 17,271 from Cole Younger when he was captured.[80] Like so many other tales of the American West, the foregoing account does not tally with other, and perhaps more reliable reports by possemen who have claimed that Cole Younger had only a Moore .32 caliber rimfire revolver in his possession when he was captured. On the other hand, Jim Younger did have a .44 Smith & Wesson Russian in his possession when he was captured.[81]

Smith & Wesson Second Model American

Smith & Wesson Second Model American

In 1873 Smith & Wesson introduced the First Model Russian. This version, although similar to the American, weighed only 38 ounces and came standard with a six inch barrel. The First Model Russian was chambered in .44 S&W, and the new .44 Russian cartridge. Why a Russian model? Unlike Colt, Smith & Wesson had not been successful in selling their revolvers to the United States Army. In order to produce their guns efficiently and in a cost-effective way they needed sales volume. The export sales to Russia, and Turkey, afforded Smith & Wesson the quantity they needed to reach a more cost effective position. There were three versions of the Russian model. Nearly 46,500 Russian Model pistols were manufactured between 1871 and 1878. John Wesley Hardin is said to have owned serial number 25,274.[82] John Wesley Hardin seemed to have owned practically every handgun made at one time or the other during his lifetime.

Matched Pair of Smith & Wesson Second Model American Revolvers.

The next improvement to be introduced by Smith & Wesson came with the development of the famous Schofield Model. There were two successive models of this revolver with total production of only 8,969. The design of the Schofield differed from the earlier S&W Models in that the latch mechanism for releasing the hinged frame was moved to the back of the frame, rather than the top of the strap that is connected to the barrel assembly. This enabled the user to open the gun with one hand and eject the spent cartridges. A man on horseback could perform this maneuver, then cradle the gun in his arm while holding the reins and reload the firearms rapidly and effectively...doing so at a full gallop. The revolver was named for Colonel George Schofield, the man who first suggested this innovation. The Schofield is one of the most highly prized and sought after firearms of the early west. Frank James is known to have carried serial numbers

3,444 and 5,476. Cole Younger carried serial number 2,341. Jesse James is known to have carried number 366, and possibly number 273 as well.[83] Famous lawmen such as Bill Tilghman favored the weapon. Frank McLowery used a Schofield at the OK Corral shootout. Lincoln County Deputy Sheriff W.H. Johnson also preferred the Schofield, and carried one while in office from 1876 until his death on 18 August 1879.

Still popular today among firearm enthusiasts, reenactors and cowboy action shooters, the only criticism of this firearm was its caliber. The Schofield is chambered in .45 Schofield, which is a slightly different cartridge configuration than the .45 Long Colt. The .45 Schofield can be loaded and fired in a Colt Model 1873 that is chambered for .45 Colt. One could not, however, safely fire the .45 Colt in the Schofield. Although one can physically load the .45 Schofield round in a Colt Model 1873, once the gun is fired the cartridge becomes firmly lodged in the cylinder and is difficult to remove without the aid of a knife blade or screwdriver. One can imagine the problem that this unfortunate event presented if it occurred during a shootout. Without a doubt there were some Schofield Model Smith & Wesson revolvers that found their way into the Lincoln County War.

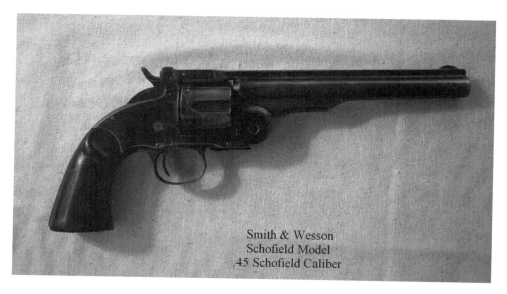

Smith & Wesson
Schofield Model
.45 Schofield Caliber

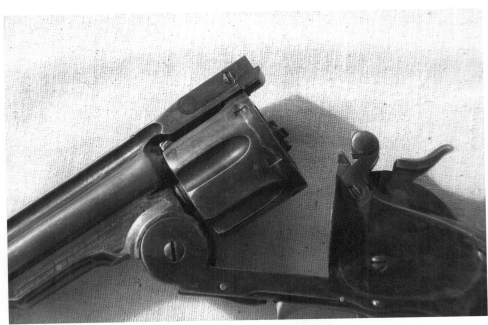

Smith & Wesson Schofield.

The last of the period "Big Iron" single action Smith & Wesson guns is the New Model Number Three. This model was introduced in 1878 and was manufactured continuously until the end of 1908. There were a total of 35,796 of these guns produced, in a variety of calibers, including many compatible with the Winchester rifle cartridge selection...such as .38-40W.C.F., .44-40 W.C.F. and .44 Henry Rimfire. Annie Oakley is said to have liked this model revolver so well that she purchased three of them.[84]

Another large caliber Smith & Wesson revolver that saw action in the Lincoln County War was the .44 Double Action, or First Model DA. This gun is the forerunner of most modern day double action Smith & Wesson revolvers, and was introduced in 1881. Before a newer model revolver replaced the First Model DA in 1913 there were 53,590 of them produced. The .44 S&W caliber was big enough to provide the stopping power required. The .44 S&W cartridge, loaded with a 200 grain bullet, launched the projectile down the barrel with a muzzle velocity of over 800 feet per second and retained 300 foot pounds of energy out to a range of 50 yards. With a complete array of popular barrel lengths available including 4, 5, 6, or 6½ inch this revolver was a handy sidekick that, because of its somewhat smaller size and reduced weight, was quick out of the holster. Unlike Colt's early attempts at a double action pistol with the unreliable Model 1877 and 1878, the Smith & Wesson product actually worked, and was not plagued by failure of the frail parts and action that had become so common an issue with the Colt. The First Model DA was a rugged handgun that stood up well under hard use. John Wesley Hardin is said to have carried serial number 352 on 19 August 1895 when he met his end at the Acme Saloon in El Paso, Texas. Hardin never had a chance to reach for that .44-40 Smith & Wesson Frontier revolver. He was felled by a surprise shot from Constable John Selman's .45 Colt Model 1873 Peacemaker.

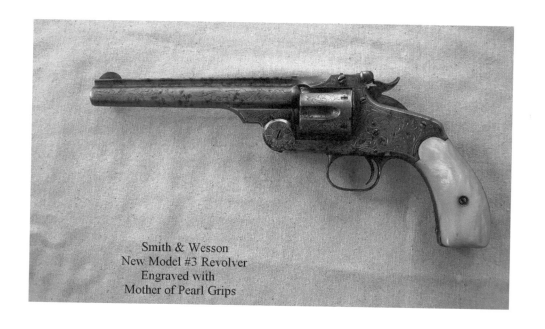

Smith & Wesson
New Model #3 Revolver
Engraved with
Mother of Pearl Grips

Smith & Wesson also produced a number of smaller pocket pistols that were often carried as a "last chance" weapon. The Models 1, 1½ and 2 were all available at the time of the Lincoln County War, but all were small caliber guns. The New Model Top Break, called the Model 1½, had just been introduced in 1878. The 1½ was chambered in the somewhat puny .32 S&W caliber, rendering it ineffective for use as anything other than a back up gun.

Smith & Wesson Model 1 1/2
.32 S&W Center Fire Caliber

If one performs a running tally of the number of Smith & Wesson large frame revolvers manufactured during this time period (1873–1881) the total is roughly 152,364 guns. By contrast, Colt produced only about 62,000 cartridge revolvers between 1873 and the start of 1881. Smith & Wesson out sold Colt by a whopping two and one half to one. Further adding to the ledger, and stacking up against Colt, were the vast number of large caliber handguns made by other reputable manufacturers of the period including Remington, Merwin Hulbert, and Harrington & Richardson. There were also a large number of Mexican, Belgian and Spanish copies of the big frame pistol, many mirroring the Colt or Smith & Wesson patent.

So why is it that practically every actor in an Old West motion picture produced before about 1980 seems to be carrying a Colt revolver? Hollywood has not let the facts get in the way of a great story. A good example of this is in Kevin Jarre's 1993 film *Tombstone.* Among the seemingly innumerable historical faux pas in this motion picture Wyatt Earp (played by Kurt Russell) is armed with a Colt Model 1873 Single Action Army with an unusually long barrel, often called the Ned Buntline Model or "Buntline Special." Earp's gun is in a holster, strapped to his hip. In reality Wyatt brought a Smith & Wesson Second Model American to the OK Corral gunfight, and he carried it in his coat pocket. Wyatt Earp may or may not have actually received a long barreled Colt Model 1873 as a gift from the prolific wild west writer Edward Zane Carrol, who used the pen name "Ned Buntline." There were a total of twenty-two long barrel Colt 1873s, referred to by most as "Buntline Specials," documented as having been produced by Colt. All of them fall in the serial number range 28,800 to 28,830, making it possible for as many as thirty-one to have actually been made. The earliest known shipments were in July and October of 1876. The largest shipment of Buntlines went to B. Kitteridge and Company of Cincinnati, Ohio. Kitteridge received four of the pistols in December 1877 and another five in March 1880. Disbelievers will claim, in chorus, that there is no reliable evidence of Ned Buntline gifting one of these special Colt revolvers to Wyatt Earp. On the other hand, believers will cite Captain Frank "Buckskin" Leslie's letter to Colt dated 14 January 1881, posted from Tombstone, Arizona, in which Leslie ordered a 12 inch barrel "Buntline Special" as their evidence. The ranks are clearly split on this controversy.[85] The author remains neutral between the warring factions.

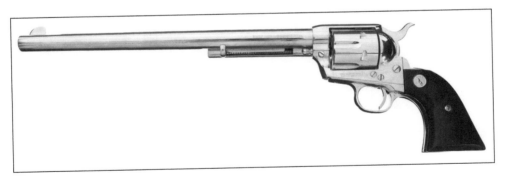

Colt Model 1873 Buntline Special

5

Other Handguns

*The optimist proclaims
that we live in the best of all possible worlds
and the pessimist fears this is true*
—James Branch Cabell

Next in line in terms of popularity after the Colt and Smith & Wesson revolvers was the Remington. Many cowboys, lawmen and outlaws favored the Remington New Model Army in .44 caliber. Remington originally produced a percussion revolver which they later converted to a cartridge firearm. For some reason, possibly as a result of the gun's popularity with Confederate soldiers during the Civil War, the Remington was especially sought after by pistoleers in the southern states and in the west. Remington made about 132,000 of their New Model Army revolvers between 1863 and 1875, and there is no estimate as to how many of them were converted to cartridge firearms before the introduction of the gun's successor, the Model 1875

Single Action. The Model 1875 was chambered in the popular .44-40 W.C.F. caliber, and was offered in 5½ inch and 7½ inch barrel lengths with either a blue or nickel finish. Remington produced about 25,000 of these revolvers between 1875 and 1889. John Wesley Hardin is known to have carried a Model 1875 Remington. The somewhat smaller Remington New Model Police conversion to .38 caliber also found its way into the hands of old west gunmen. About 18,000 of these guns were manufactured before production ceasing in 1873.

Perhaps the most noted, and easily recognizable of the Remington handguns is the Remington Double Derringer. This little gun has two barrels chambered in .41 caliber rimfire, and the barrels are only three inches long. The derringer has a pivot hinge, allowing the gun to be opened for loading and unloading. There were 150,000 of these small pocket pistols manufactured between 1866 and 1935. The Double Derringer is an immensely popular gun, and one that is still prized by collectors. Due to their small size they could be conveniently concealed in a vest or coat pocket. Remington also made several other models of pocket pistol including the Remington-Elliot in .41 caliber rimfire single shot, the Remington-Smoot revolver in .30 caliber rimfire and the tiny Iroquois model in .22 caliber rimfire.[86]

Remington New Model Army

Forehand & Wadsworth began to produce a line of large frame cartridge revolver beginning in about 1875. Their offering was chambered in the popular .44 Russian caliber. These guns looked very much like the Smith & Wesson New Model 3 and were called the New Model Army. They were available in 6½ inch barrel only, and were all six shot capacity revolvers.

Forehand & Wadsworth 1st Model Army .44 Cal.

In 1875 Hopkins & Allen offered a .44 caliber rimfire six shot, big frame revolver. Their version came in 4½ inch, 6 inch and 7½ inch barrel lengths, and was marked "XL No 8." The Hopkins & Allen pistol was extremely popular. Merwin Hulbert & Company of New York City actually had their guns manufactured by Hopkins & Allen of Norwich,

Connecticut. Merwin & Hulbert offered their big frame model called the Army in .44-40 W.C.F. and .44 Merwin & Hulbert calibers. The barrel length was seven inch. Later on a shorter barreled version was added to their list of options. The early models lacked a top strap connecting the front and rear of the frame over the top of the cylinder, like the early Colt of 1872. Later models had this feature, and were also offered in a double action version. Production of these guns began in about 1875. There was a pocket model available as well, but it was not introduced until the early 1880s. The Merwin & Hulbert was a very sturdy and well made firearm. Without a doubt some of these found their way into the hands of Lincoln County War combatants.

The final category of handguns is the derringers. There were a vast number of models and manufacturers who produced a variety of guns in a broad array of calibers. Some of these guns were reliable and others were not. The bad ones were the origin of the term *hotter than a two-dollar pistol*. This expression referred to the fact that many of the inexpensive, poorly manufactured pocket guns would become hot to the touch after firing just one shot. Colt made a line of derringers, as did Sharps, Remington and numerous other makers. Vest pocket size guns in large calibers were good weapons for "last line of defense" situations. John Tunstall is known to have carried a Forehand & Wadsworth British Bulldog in caliber .455 Webley.[87] Colt made three models of these large calibers guns in .41 caliber and produced about 45,000 of them between 1870 and 1912. Perhaps as many as four to five thousand were in circulation by the time of the Lincoln County War. It would stand to reason that some of these guns would have found their way into the Lincoln County War.

Merwin & Hulbert Frontier Model .44-40 W.C.F.

6

The Winchester

The Gun That Won the West.

In the dialogue of many old west motion pictures one frequently hear someone remark "...he grabbed his Winchester." One practically never hears someone exclaim, "...he grabbed his Marlin...or he grabbed his Spencer."

As a practical matter the word Winchester became synonymous with the word gun in the old west. The ever present and always reliable Winchester is seen poking out of saddle scabbards throughout the photographic history of the American West. Even as late as the turn of the last century, after so many other quality long guns had been introduced, the Winchester remained the gold standard of weapons. Texas Ranger Captain John H. Rogers inventoried the weaponry of his Company of Rangers midway through 1899 and noted, "...4 Winchester carbines Model 1873, .44 caliber; 2 Marlin rifles Model 1893, .30-30 caliber; 1 Marlin rifle in .38-42 caliber and another .32-40; and 2 Winchester shotguns, a 10 and a 12 gauge."[88]

Practically every self respecting gun hand of the old west had a Winchester. The predecessor of the Winchester, the Henry rifle, was first produced on 8 August 1854.[89] There were 12,475 Henry rifles assembled between 1860 and 1866. The Henry saw service in the Civil War. The Union Army purchased 1,731 of them. Although the Henry saw limited duty during the war, it is credited with saving the lives of thousands of Union troops during the Battle of Chickamauga where the retreating Union Army was saved by just 535 men armed with Henry rifles. The Henry rifle proved itself on the western frontier as well. On 21 December 1866 a party of eight woodcutters left Fort Laramie in Wyoming Territory, near present day Sheridan, in north central Wyoming. The group was soon ambushed by a sizeable band of Sioux Indians. Two civilians in the group of Cavalry soldiers, James Wheatley and Isaac Fisher, were armed with Henry rifles. Together with the soldiers they managed to hold off the initial raiding party until help arrived. The rapid fire performance of the Henry compared to that of the single shot carbines carried by the soldiers made a profound difference in the fight. Unfortunately when Captain William Fetterman rescued the woodcutting party with a detachment of Cavalry soldiers he was lured into an ambush. An estimated two thousand Sioux Indians surrounded the group, and after a fight that lasted about forty minutes all eighty soldiers and civilians were massacred. This encounter, called "The Fetterman Fight," was soon followed by a similar incident called "The Wagon Box Fight" which took place on 2 August 1867.[90]

Henry Rifle

The design of the Henry was improved upon with the introduction of the Model 1866 on 22 May 1866. Both the Henry and the Model 1866 fired the .44 Henry rimfire cartridge. It is claimed that the Plains Indians of the west first called the Model 1866 Winchester the "Yellowboy," presumably for its bright brass receiver. The origin of the term is not that important, but the nickname has stuck with the gun over the years and is still used today. It was the Henry rifle that one Confederate soldier of the American Civil War described as being "...that infernal rifle that you can load on Sunday and shoot all week..." They were referring to the fact that the Henry held up to sixteen rounds in the tubular magazine beneath the barrel. The receiver of the Henry, and the Model 1866, are actually bronze, not brass. The Model 1866 was originally chambered in the .44 Henry rimfire cartridge, and was a huge improvement over other cartridge long arms of the era. It was also a well designed and functioning lever action repeating weapon. The Model 1866 fired a 200 grain semi-pointed or flat nosed lead bullet that was propelled by twenty eight grains of black powder. The "66" as it was called came standard with a 24 inch octagon or round barrel on rifles and a 20 inch round barrel on carbines. After serial number 100,000 longer barrels up to as long as 36 inch could be ordered on rifles. Extra heavy barrels were available after serial number 150,000. The Model 1866 magazine had a capacity of seventeen rounds, and the carbine thirteen. In the hands of an experienced operator the Winchester Carbine was a very effective rapid fire weapon. Buckshot Roberts displayed this at Blazer's Mill when he emptied his Winchester carbine of all thirteen rounds in short order, wounding five men and seriously injuring two of them.[91] There were a total of 156,540 Model 1866s manufactured between 1866 and 1898, and practically 137,000 of them were made before the start of the Lincoln County War. Without question some of the participants of the Lincoln County War used the Yellowboy.

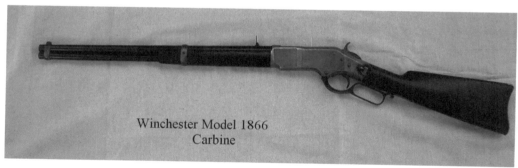

Winchester Model 1866 Carbine

Winchester Model 1866 Rifle

Winchester Model 1866
Carbine

Winchester Model 1866 Carbine

By 1873 Oliver Winchester had improved on his design and introduced the Model of 1873. The 1873 was first available in the improved .44-40 W.C.F. cartridge. The .44-40 W.C.F. designation means a .44 caliber projectile that was propelled down the barrel by 40 grains of black powder. The term W.C.F. means Winchester Center Fire. This cartridge proved to be an excellent one, and is still widely used today. The model 1873 had many design improvements beyond just the enhanced caliber selection. The receiver was now made of steel to handle the more powerful .44-40 cartridge. There was a dust cover over the previously open receiver to prevent dirt and foreign objects from fouling the mechanism. Like the 1866, the standard barrel length for carbines was 20 inch and 24 inch for rifles. Round or octagon barrels were offered as standard on rifles. Later on a part round/part octagon version was available, as was a heavy "bull barrel." Winchester offered a vast array of options that could be ordered individually or in combination. Some of the most popular selections on this list of options included; short magazine, checkered butt stock and forearm, deluxe wood, special sights, engraving, shotgun butt stock, sling swivels and pistol grip stock. The Model 1873 was eventually offered in several calibers, but during the time of the Lincoln County War the .44-40 was the only choice. In 1881 the .38-40 W.C.F. caliber was introduced, and a few guns in this caliber could have found their way into the hands of Pat Garrett's posse or by the time Dirty Dave Rudabaugh broke out of the Las Vegas jail on 31 December 1881.

The Model 1873 has been called *The Gun That Won the West*. That classification was accurately applied. The "73" is highly prized by collectors today. During the late 1800s and early 1900s it was one of the most sought after and valuable of the Winchester stable of firearms. There were about 27,000 Winchester 1873s manufactured before the Lincoln County War began. That total reached practically 82,000 by the time the war had ended. Production of this model continued until 1923 and nearly 750,000 were made.

Frequent reference is made to the Winchester rifle in accounts of the various events of the Lincoln County War. Photographs of the period depict Winchester 1873 carbines in the hands of numerous participants, including Billy the Kid.[92] When Mrs. Casey, by then a widow, decided to return to Texas in October 1877 and take with her a quantity of horses and cattle that she had stolen from John Tunstall, Dick Brewer,

John Middleton and four other men headed out after her in pursuit. The group picked the best of the remaining Tunstall horses and loaded their gear, including five new Winchester carbines that John Tunstall had just received at the store as they headed out for Texas.

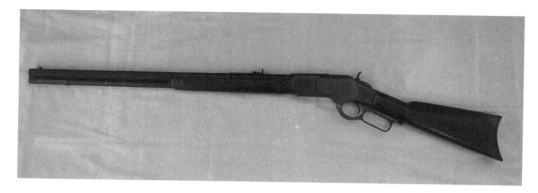

Winchester Model 1873 Rifle.

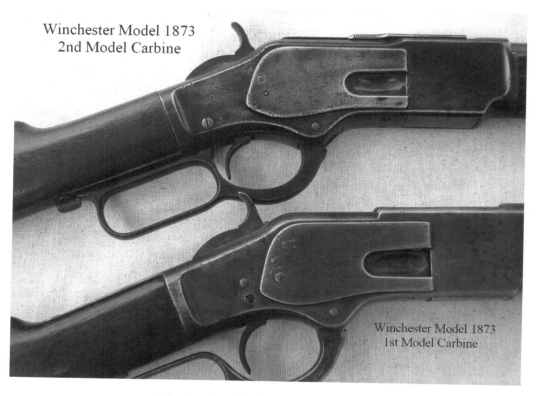

Winchester Model 1873 Receivers.

If one conducts an examination of a period Model 1873 to determine if it could have been used during the Lincoln County War a good place to begin is with the weapon's serial number. Guns between number between 1 and number 27,502 were made before the Five Day Siege at the McSween house. Guns between serial number 27,503 and 81,621 were made afterwards, but before Billy was killed at Fort Sumner. The serial number appears on the bottom of the tang, beneath the lever. If one is unable to pick up the gun to examine it (for example in a museum) there are several visible differences between the 1st and 2nd model 1873 that are shown in the photographs that follow. First, there is a difference in the location and number of screws and pins in the side of the receiver. Most obvious is the shape of the dust cover, and the knurled "thumbprint." It is significantly different on the 1st model than on any subsequent iteration. Lastly the front and rear sights are significantly different. There are a number of other less profound differences between the various models of the 1873 Winchester, but the foregoing are the most obvious. By examining the dust cover alone one should be able to determine the weapon's relative age. There is a series of photographs (from the author's collection) that follows illustrating the differences between the 1st Model and the 2nd and 3rd model. In all of these photos the 2nd model carbine is at the top of the photo and the 1st model is at the bottom photo.

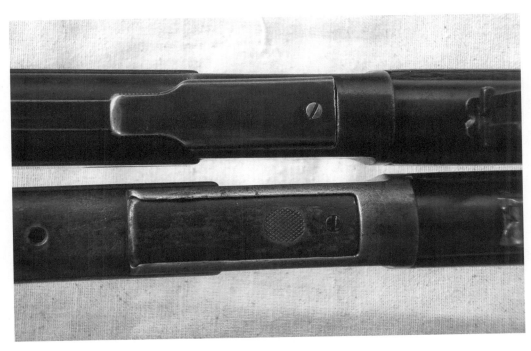

Winchester Model 1873 Dust Covers.

The Winchester had little competition at the time. Colt did not introduce their line of repeating rifles until 1883 with their short lived Burgess lever action model. Production of the Burgess was a mere 6,403 guns, and ended by 1885. Later Colt introduced their Lightning series long gun. The small and medium frame Lightning Rifles were introduced in 1884. The large frame version was introduced later, in 1887. The Lightning was a pump action gun as opposed to a lever action. It was more expensive to produce than the Winchester and a bit more difficult to maintain and clean. The Lightning was an outstanding gun, but unfortunately its popularity faded over time. Marlin also introduced a long gun to compete with the Winchester. Their offering was the Model of 1881, which was chambered in a variety of calibers. Like the Colt Lightning, it was introduced too late to be of any importance with respect to the Lincoln County War.

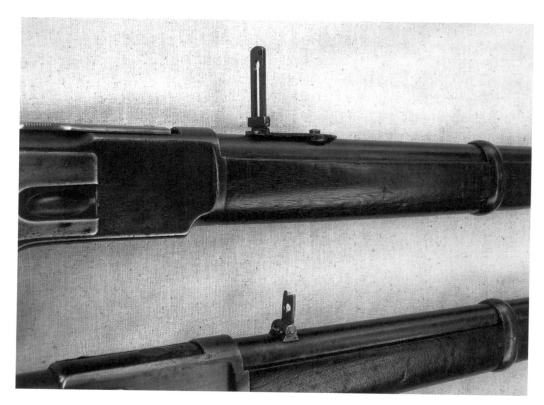

Winchester Model 1873 Rear Sights.

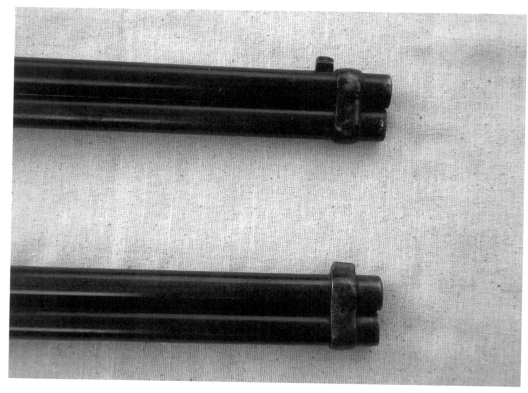

Winchester Model 1873 Front Sights.

60

In the only authenticated photograph of Charlie Bowdre and his wife Manuela, Charlie is pictured with a seemingly oversized Winchester rifle and a large cartridge belt, called a "prairie belt" containing some pretty massive cartridges.[93] Bowdre's Winchester is frequently misidentified as a Model 1873. It is not. The gun is a Model 1876, or "Centennial Model" in the somewhat rare carbine configuration. The Model 1876 is significantly larger, and heavier, than the 1873 and is chambered for much larger cartridges. Of the 63,871 Model 1876s produced between 1876 and 1898 fewer than 10,000 were carbines. Almost one third of them had been manufactured before Billy was killed in 1881.[94] The Model 1876 was offered in a number of more powerful calibers, such as the .45-70 Government, .45-75-350, the 50-95 and 50-110 Express. The .45-75 was a 350 grain bullet, almost half the size of the .45-70 government round which weighed a whopping 405 grains. Such calibers delivered twice the energy of the .44-40 W.C.F. round in the smaller Model 1873. For example, the .45-70 bullet had a muzzle velocity of over 1,300 feet per second and retained about 1,000 foot pounds of energy at 200 yards! Considering the earlier example of stopping power where roughly 300 foot pounds of energy has been set by some as a benchmark, it is apparent that the range of these larger caliber rifles was considerable. The Model 1876 rifle came standard with a 28 inch barrel in octagon or round. The magazine held twelve big bore cartridges. Barrel lengths up to 36 inch were offered. The 1876 was popular among hunters since it packed the punch needed for big game, for open country, and for long range shooting. The legendary Tom Horn preferred a Winchester Model 1876 in caliber .45-60. Later in life Horn favored the improved, smokeless powder Model 1894. His Model 1894 was a full round barrel, half magazine .30-30 W.C.F., serial number 82,667. It was shipped from the factory on 19 June 1900.

The Model of 1876 was the last of the Winchesters that was available before the end of 1881. In total, roughly 252,000 Winchesters of various models and calibers were made before the end of the Lincoln County War.[95]

Winchester Model 1876 Rifle.

Winchester Model 1876

Winchester Model 1876 Rifle.

7

Other Long Guns

*Small opportunities
are often the beginning of great enterprises.*
—Demosthenes

During the 1800s the array of long guns available was immense. One could fill the pages of a sizeable book with a complete accounting of them all. Many were developed near the end of the Civil War, or shortly afterwards. Most were single shot weapons. Apart from the Colt, Marlin and Winchester rifles perhaps the two most significant in terms of their impact on the Lincoln County War were the Sharps and the Spencer repeaters.

Christian Sharps produced a line of fine firearms during and just after the Civil War.[96] Sharps' first significant creations were the Model of 1859, Model of 1863 and Model of 1865. All were produced in rifle and carbine configurations. The carbines had 22 inch barrels and the military rifles 30 inch barrels. All were originally made in .52 caliber percussion breechloaders, but over 32,000 were converted to metallic cartridge firearms firing the .52-70 round. The Model 1869 rifle and carbine was offered in caliber .44-77, .50-70 and .60 caliber. Production of this model totaled less than 1,000. The most famous Sharps "far shooter" is the Model of 1874. The Creedmore Models, the Sporting Model and the Long Range Model top the list of sought after Sharps firearms. Doc Scurlock's brother-in-law, Fernando Herrera, shot Charlie "Lallycooler" Crawford at a great distance during the Five Day Siege with a Sharps rifle in caliber 45-120-555.[97] Production of the 1874 model is estimated to have been as high as 12,000 to 13,000 if one considers all of the various configurations. The Sharps was, and continues to be, an extremely popular weapon for long range shooting. The Sharps rifle was made famous by its reliability and performance. In one such case during the Second Battle of Adobe Walls in 1874 a seemingly impossible shot was made with a Sharps rifle at a range that is impressive by today's standards. On what is believed to have been the third or fourth day of siege a small group of Indians had ventured to the edge of distant ridge to plan their next attack. At the urging of one of the other buffalo hunters a member of the group named Billy Dixon, who was known as a crack shot, took aim with a fifty caliber Sharps rifle that he had borrowed from the Hanrahan Store (either a .50-70 or .50-90). The hunters laughed at Dixon, exclaiming, "they're a mile away!" Undaunted, Dixon took careful aim, squeezed the trigger, and watched as the tiny figure of an Indian in the distance, mounted on his horse, tumbled to the ground dead. It was this act that caused the Indians to become so discouraged that they gave up the fight and left. Two weeks later a team of U.S. Army surveyors under the command of Nelson A. Miles measured the distance of the shot and recorded it to have been 1,538 yards—or nine-tenths of a mile. For the remainder of his life Billy Dixon never claimed that the shot was anything other than a lucky one. His memoirs do not even devote a full paragraph to *the shot.*

Next is the Spencer Repeating Rifle (and carbine) which were manufactured in Boston, Massachusetts. Production of the Spencer began before the Civil War.[98] The early models were in .52 caliber rimfire. The post war models were offered in .56-52 or .56-50 caliber. There were nearly 150,000 of these guns made. After the war the Model 1865 and Model 1867 were produced in .50 caliber rimfire, and about 33,000 of the two models were made. The Spencer was a popular weapon, featuring a tubular magazine in the butt stock that held seven rounds.

Because of its use by Buckshot Roberts at the Blazer's Mill shootout we can't leave out the old standby Springfield Model 1873 Trapdoor Model.[99] The mortally wounded Roberts, out of ammunition for his Winchester, picked up a Model 1873 Springfield from the home of Dr. Blazer and made an outstanding shot of 125 yards. His bullet struck Dick Brewer in the right eye, killing him instantly. The Model 1873 Springfield was produced between 1873 and 1877. A total of about 73,000 were manufactured. The Springfield rifle was a large weapon that weighed 9 pounds 8 ounces and came with a barrel that measured 32 5/8 inches in length. The gun fired the Government .45-70 caliber cartridge, and was loaded one round at a time through a trap door breech mechanism. The Springfield was also available in and carbine model with a 22 inch barrel. These guns were accurate at distances in excess of 1,000 yards, and were favored by buffalo hunters for their long distance accuracy and knock down power. Buffalo Bill Cody used a Springfield 1873 Model for years, and affectionately named it after the ruthless renaissance Italian noblewoman Lucrezia Borgia. Cody's Springfield hangs over a doorway in the Buffalo Bill Museum in Cody, Wyoming.

Mention of the Model 1873 Springfield also causes one to recall the "Bobbie Cain" photo. A part of the Altermann and Wiggins Collection, the caption on the photo reads, "Local rancher's son Bobbie Cain looking over a rifle belonging to the La Paloma Bar. This gun, part of the bar's collection, was left in San Patricio by Billy the Kid on his way to Fort Sumner shortly before his death." The photo depicts a lad of perhaps ten years of age holding a full stock 1873 Springfield Trapdoor rifle. Being a skeptic by nature I am inclined to reject the foregoing claim of provenance. It seems so completely out of character for Billy to arm himself with such a massive piece of iron that only fired one shot at a time. We know from numerous testimonies that Billy favored the Winchester 1873 carbine (or Whitney Kennedy carbine). Some historians have speculated that perhaps this is the rifle that Buckshot Roberts used at Blazer's Mill when he killed Dick Brewer, and that over time the claim

of ownership of this gun was "enhanced." Although a skeptic, I am a hopeless romantic and would like to believe that this particular old Springfield may actually be the one that was used at Blazer's Mill.

Although the Whitney Kennedy was not as popular as the Winchester it was the second favorite lever action long gun of Billy the Kid, and thus merits inclusion if only for that reason. Andrew Burgess was a well known Civil War photographer, designer of fire alarms and prolific designer of weapons. Burgess boasted having logged nearly 600 firearm patents. He approached Whitney with his unique design for a lever action repeating rifle, magazine fed, and chambered in the enormous .45-70 Government cartridge. It was Whitney's hope that this gun would be accepted in the military trials of 1878, and would be adopted as a repeating rifle for the military. Although not successful, Whitney continued production of the gun in sporting and military versions. It is believed by some that Whitney may have contracted to manufacture as few as 2,000 of the weapons. In 1880 Samuel V. Kennedy and Frank W. Tiesing redesigned the 1878 Burgess rifle to accept the much smaller .44-40 Winchester Center Fire cartridge. With the basic machining already in place the transition to the smaller cartridge was rather inexpensive. The last Burgess was shipped from the factory in March 1880. The first Whitney Kennedy was also shipped in March 1880. The gun was produced in rifle and carbine configuration, and was made from 1880 until early 1886. Total production is estimated to have been about 23,500.

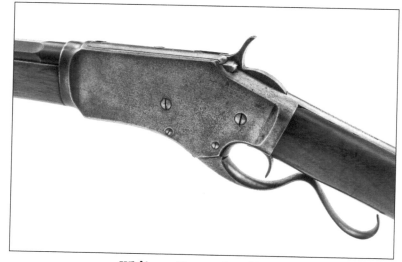

Whitney Kennedy Rifle

There were a vast number of long guns available during the Lincoln County War. The Winchester, Sharps, and Spencer comprised only a small portion of them. There is a long list of "all others" that may have been carried by a few combatants, but most seem to have been armed with a Winchester. Keep in mind that both factions had a dry goods store with an ample stock of firearms and ammunition at their disposal. I doubt that any of the principal characters in the saga went about begging for a good firearm.

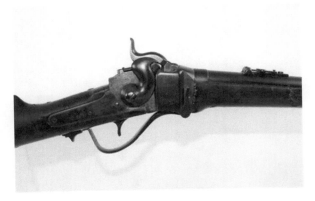

Sharps Carbine.

Spencer Carbine.

8

The Shotguns

*For those times when
any old firearm just won't do...!*

Practically nothing will send a chill up one's spine more quickly than looking at the business end of a double barrel shotgun. An imposing weapon in the hands of man, woman or child, the shotgun was the favored weapon of most ranchers, as well as many lawmen and outlaws. A tally of Texas lawmen that were killed during the 1800s reveals that fully sixty percent were killed by an assailant who was armed with a shotgun. One need not be wealthy to own one, nor be an especially accomplished marksman to be effective in their use. Perhaps the only significant drawback to the shotgun was its somewhat limited range of effectiveness. Farmers and ranchers used the shotgun as a "game getter."[100] A blast of lead pellets fired from a shotgun was effective for taking small game, waterfowl, and larger game at close range. When loaded with heavier shot the weapon was extremely effective when used against an adversary.

A complete list of the shotguns that were available at the time of the Lincoln County War would be an epic task to produce. Suffice it to say that there were a vast number of them available. Manuel "The Indian" Segovia used a shotgun to dispatch Frank McNab at the Fritz Ranch. Billy the Kid used Bob Olinger's shotgun against him during Billy's escape from the Lincoln County courthouse on 28 April 1881. There are several other documented accounts of the use of a shotgun in the annals of the Lincoln County War, but to my knowledge only the Bob Olinger gun has been identified by brand and gauge.

As cited earlier, the shotgun is a very effective short-range weapon. It is deadly at a range of forty yards or less, and at greater distances when used against fowl or small game. The principal purpose of the shotgun is hunting birds and small game. Unlike the rifle or handgun, which fire single projectiles, a shotgun fires a charge of several small lead pellets called shot that can range in size from smaller than grains of rice to as large as a garden pea. The pellets are contained in a cartridge case called a shell, which is much larger than the case used for rifle or pistol ammunition. The quantity of pellets contained in the shotgun shell depends upon the size of the lead shot used. The lead pellets when propelled down the barrel spread into a pattern that widens as the distance increases and covers an area perhaps three feet in diameter with small fragments of lead shot. The greater the distance from the barrel that the shot travels the larger the distance between pellets becomes...and the less energy that remains. A bird can literally fly through the pattern of small lead shot if one attempts to shoot at too great a distance. With heavier size pellets like "buckshot" there may be as few as nine or eleven pellets in a load.

The term "buckshot" was coined when heavier size pellets were created for use in killing deer. Lead shot size is measured by an interesting scale, beginning with the smallest, number 12 having a diameter of .05 of an inch and ending with the largest which is called 000, Buck having a diameter of .36 of an inch. This unusual scale of measurement advances from 12 to 9, then 8½, 8, 7½, 6, 5, 4, 2, then BB, Buck, 4 Buck, 3 Buck, 2 Buck, 1 Buck, 0 Buck, 00 Buck and finally 000 Buck.

Readily available, simple to operate, deadly, and cheap to buy. An excellent combination that was good for frontier use. If a household had only one gun it was probably a shotgun. The shotgun is another example of where Hollywood has led us down the dark path of ignorance and misinformation. Seldom does an old west motion picture contain a scene depicting anyone other than the stagecoach guard with a shotgun. Further, in almost every case the stagecoach guard has a shotgun with a short barrel. In reality most shotguns did not have their barrels shortened, and not all stagecoach guards carried shotguns. Many outlaws and cowboys were armed with a shotgun. They were vastly more effective and easier to aim at short range. The damage that can be inflicted on a human by receiving the brunt of a shotgun blast at short range is truly profound. On the down side, even with a double barrel shotgun one has only two shots...then reloading is required. Reloading is not a complicated or time consuming process, but if one is facing down a man with a Winchester who has sixteen rounds in the magazine of his weapon the person with the shotgun is at a decided disadvantage. Furthermore, the shotgun is largely ineffective in man to man combat beyond fifty or sixty yards.

Components of a Shotgun Shell

Nonetheless, there were unquestionably many shotguns used in the Lincoln County War. One of the brands thought to be superior, and highly prized, was the W.W. Greener. The Greener is made in England. It is an exceptionally well made gun, and was offered in a variety of grades depending upon ones taste and budget. By 1874 there were a vast number of Greener shotguns in the United States. Both Wyatt Earp and Doc Holliday are said to have owned Greener shotguns. According to Graham Greener, the current director of the company, both guns were special ordered and made to the respective men's specifications. Holliday is claimed by some to have carried his 10 gauge double barrel lever lock Greener at the OK Corral gunfight, which City Marshal Virgil Earp handed off to him before the shooting commenced.[101] However, the best information available at this time is that Virgil Earp picked up a Meteor brand shotgun from the Wells Fargo office on the way to the fight and handed it off to Holliday.[102] The only area of old west study that is perhaps more contentious than the Lincoln County War and Billy the Kid is the OK Corral gunfight. For that reason alone the author offers Graham Greener's claim with regard to Wyatt Earp and Doc Holliday's ownership of Greener shotguns for the reader's conjecture.

Although the barrels of shotguns were sometimes shortened, or "sawed off", this practice was far less prevalent than Hollywood would have one believe. Most shotguns came standard with barrel of 28, 30, 32 or 34 inch lengths. Usually when someone shortened a shotgun in the late 1800s the barrel length was reduced to 20 or perhaps 22 inch. Rarely did anyone shorten one to 18 inches or less.

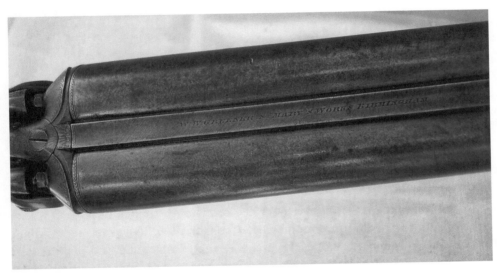

W.W. Greener Shotgun (top of barrel).

Many period shotguns were contract manufactured, thus one could have one's own name as a brand name if so desired. The American Arms Company of Boston, and others, would private brand guns for you if one ordered a large enough quantity. Large stores and distributors such as Hartley & Graham, Sears and Montgomery Wards did so frequently. This practice added to the hundreds of brands that were manufactured during the late 1800s and early 1900s. Some of the more popular brands of this period include Remington, Ithaca, Baker, Colt, Crescent, Charles Daly, Eli Whitney, Fox, Forehand & Wadsworth, Harrington & Richardson, Hunter, Iver Johnson, Lefever, Marlin, Parker, L.C. Smith, and Stevens. Most of these guns were double barrel weapons, produced in a variety of gauges, but the 16, 12 or 10 gauge were most prevalent. As a rule, shotguns produced before 1890 had a Damascus steel barrel. A Damascus barrel was produced by winding a steel wire around a mandrel, then forge welding it into shape. These barrels were decidedly less sturdy than their modern counterparts, but were adequate for the black powder loads of the day that did not produce anywhere near the chamber pressure of the smokeless gunpowder of today.

W.W. Greener Shotgun
Double Barrel 12 Gauge

W.W. Greener Shotgun.

Unlike the process for measuring a rifle or pistol the gauge or bore of a shotgun is measured in a very different manner. The measurement logic may seem a bit odd, but a "12 gauge" means that one can make 12 lead balls, each of equal diameter to the gun barrel, out of 1 pound of lead. This instrumentality of measurement originated in the days when one would buy lead by the pound, and makes one's own ammunition.

Thus the lowly shotgun, inexpensive to own and fire, versatile, and deadly at close range played a vital role in the Lincoln County War.

9

The Guns of John Henry Tunstall

*Don't place too much confidence
in the man who boasts of being as honest
as the day is long.
Wait until you meet him at night*
—Robert C. Edwards

John Henry Tunstall was born on 6 March 1853. His family lived in a three-story brick home on Queensbridge Road in Dalston, London. Dalston was at the time an affluent section of London. His father was John Partridge Tunstall, listed on the birth certificate as a "professional traveler." His mother was Emily Ramie, the daughter of a wealthy Channel Island family. Emily had married John Partridge when she was just nineteen and he was thirty-four. Little is known of John Partridge Tunstall, but it is apparent that he was something of a well to do businessman and was employed at Copestake, Crampton & Co. Ltd at the time of John Henry's birth. The 1870 census records for John Partridge show him to have a business at 8 Bow Churchyard called J.P. Tunstall & Co. Shippers. The Tunstalls had five children in total; Emily Francis, Clara, John Henry, Lilian and Mabel. Clara died in 1863. John Henry was five feet eleven inches tall and weighed a mere 138 pounds when he left home in 1872. He had sandy hair, was clean-shaven, and was blind in his right eye from some accident or illness, we do not know which. He usually dressed in a business suit or at times of leisure in a Harris Tweed rough suit.[103]

In August of 1872 John Henry Tunstall boarded the Cunard ocean liner *Calabria*, which he described as "a very fine machine" and headed to Victoria, British Columbia, Canada by way of New York and San Francisco. When his stay in San Francisco had concluded he boarded a packet ship for the short trip up the coast to Victoria, British Columbia, Canada where he would spend about two years working at the firm of Turner, Beeton, and Tunstall, Ltd., a business in which his father was a partner. It soon became obvious to John that he would not make his fortune in such a way, given a wage of $60 a month. He also found his employer to be critical of his work and impossible to tolerate. Tunstall departed for New Mexico by way of San Francisco, arriving in Santa Fe on 15 August 1876 and in Lincoln on 6 November 1876. The events of his brief 567 days in Lincoln would leave a lasting mark on history.

John Henry Tunstall, *Courtesy of Robert McCubbin, Santa Fe, New Mexico*

The 1970 Andrew Fenady motion picture "Chisum" portrayed John Tunstall as a man of about seventy years of age, a pipe smoker, and as someone who did not carry a gun. In truth John Tunstall detested smoke, was very accomplished with firearms, and was just shy of his twenty fifth birthday when he was assassinated. We know for certain that John Henry Tunstall owned several firearms, and by all accounts he was accomplished in their use in spite of the fact that he had lost the vision in his right eye. There are reports of Tunstall shooting "... his Winchester..." while he was in Victoria, British Columbia, Canada, and again in California in 1876. Once he had established his store in Lincoln he had access to the latest in firearms that Colt, Winchester, and many other manufacturers had to offer. From his own correspondence with his family, and from physical evidence that has survived, we know that John Tunstall owned a Colt Model 1873 Single Action Army revolver chambered in .45 Long Colt caliber. It is serial number 28,190. The gun has a 7½ inch barrel, a nickel finish and one piece wood grips.[104] This is also the gun that, by some accounts, Tom Hill used to deliver a fatal shot to the head of John Tunstall on 18 February 1878 (although the veracity of that claim is challenged to some extent by the post mortem report by Dr. Apell).

Tunstall was also known to own "...a large caliber pocket pistol." There is documentation to support the fact that he brought a British Bulldog revolver with him when he left England. By one account he fired a few shots with that gun in the forest near Niagara Falls to impress a girl he had met while en route to British Columbia traveling on a Northern Pacific Railroad train from New York and San Francisco. That firearm, a Forehand & Wadsworth Bulldog chambered in caliber .455 Webley is a six shot revolver with a 2 3/8 inch barrel. It was purchased in 1927 by a man named Leman and is presently in a private collection in Ruidoso, New Mexico. The Forehand & Wadsworth Bulldog is truly a powerful little handgun that was easy to conceal in a coat pocket.

Forehand & Wadsworth Bulldog .455 Webley.

Colt Single Action Army 7½" Barrel w/ One Piece Wood Grips.

10

The Guns of Sheriff Patrick Floyd Jarvis Garrett

How fortune brings to earth the oversure!
—Francesco Petrarca Petrarch

Patrick Floyd Jarvis Garrett, oldest son of John Lumpkin and Elizabeth Ann Jarvis, was born in Claiborne Parish, Louisiana, near Homer on 5 June 1850. On 25 January 1869 he left Louisiana and went to Dallas County, Texas where he worked as a cowboy from 1875 to 1877. Next he joined W. Skelton Glenn as a buffalo hunter in the Texas Panhandle where he killed Joe Briscoe in a disagreement (reportedly over buffalo hides). Garrett was an imposing figure with piercing blue eyes, standing an extraordinary six feet four inches tall. In 1878 he moved to Fort Sumner and worked in Beaver Smith's saloon while at the same time raising hogs. Garrett married Juanita Gutierrez in 1879. She died before the end of the year. On 14 January 1880 he married Apolonaria (or Polonaria), the twenty one year old daughter of Jose Gutierres. This marriage produced eight children, the last being Jarvis Garrett who died 20 May 1991.

On 7 November 1880 Pat Garrett was appointed Lincoln County Sheriff, taking over for Sheriff George Kimbrell who he had bested in the open election. His first goal as sheriff was to catch Billy the Kid. Garrett left Lincoln almost immediately after his election, and several weeks before his actual appointment as sheriff took effect. On 19 December 1880, Garrett killed Tom Folliard who was said to have been Billy's closest friend and constant companion. A few nights later his posse captured Billy, Dave Rudabaugh, Billy Wilson, and Tom Pickett. During the same encounter, Garrett mistakenly shot Charley Bowdre thinking he was Billy.

Bonney was tried and convicted. After suffering poor treatment at the hand of jailer Bob Olinger Bonney escaped from the jail on 28 April 1881 after killing Olinger and his deputy James Bell. Garrett and his posse tracked Bonney to the home of Pete Maxwell near Fort Sumner where, on 14 July 1881, Garrett shot and killed Bonney.

After his term as sheriff ended Garrett turned his hand to ranching. With the not so capable assistance of Ash Upson he wrote a book about Billy the Kid. Garrett's book came out in 1882, after eight other books on the same topic had beaten him to press. Garrett moved to Uvalde, Texas, where he became county commissioner in 1889. He returned to New Mexico and was hired to investigate the mysterious death of Albert J. Fountain. On 7 October of 1899 Garrett was appointed sheriff of Dona Ana County, New Mexico. Next he became Customs Collector in El Paso, Texas in 1901 under an appointment by President Theodore Roosevelt. That proved to be another failed venture, spoiled in large part by his excessive drinking and belligerence. After a two year term his appointment was not renewed. Garrett returned to ranching in Dona Ana County. His last two years were troubled ones, filled with personal and business difficulties. On 29 February 1908 he was shot to death while traveling to Las Cruces with Carl Adamson and Jesse Wayne Brazel. Brazel confessed to the killing and was acquitted on the grounds that it was self defense. There are those who believe that Garrett was shot from ambush by the notorious James "Killing Jim" Miller. Miller is said to have been paid in cattle to perform the execution. However, more recently some have argued that Garrett's real killer was Archie Prentice "Print" Rhode. After Garrett's murder Rhode removed to Yavapai County, Arizona where he purchased a ranch.[105]

Garrett was buried in the Odd Fellows Cemetery in Roswell on 5 March 1908 alongside his daughter Ida who died in 1896.

Garrett was not a very likeable character, so it is ironic that there are more guns linked to him than there are to any of the other participants in the Lincoln County War. Perhaps that is because he lived longer than many, and was famous for his deeds during his own lifetime.

Pat Garrett is believed to have owned several

Winchester rifles and carbines, but one that can be specifically attributed to him is a Winchester 1873 rifle. The gun is serial number 31,829 and was manufactured by Winchester and shipped from the factory on 21 February 1879. When it was shipped it was a standard 24 inch octagon barrel rifle with a plain trigger. It is a caliber .44-40 W.C.F. rifle, and according to the Cody Firearms Museum records was one of a 100 gun shipment to an unrecorded address in Texas. I am familiar with the Winchester records that reside at the Cody Firearms Museum and it would be highly unlikely for the records to contain any more specific information than the foregoing. Someone shortened the barrel of this gun to twelve inches at some point during its life. The gun now belongs to the Staley family, who purchased it from Cipriano and Florentino Baca. It had apparently been in the Lincoln County Sheriff's Armory from 1879 until 28 April 1881 and was said to have been confiscated from the outlaw Frank Wheeler.

The current owner claims that the gun was shortened by a gunsmith named Henry Kimball of Tascosa, Texas. Chris Hirsch's book "The Texas Gun Trade" has no listing for a Henry Kimball in Tascosa, or anywhere else in Texas. No information to support this claim has been offered by the gun's owner, and I am inclined to disbelieve their claim concerning the gun's alterations. I think the gun was in its original 24 inch configuration when the Bacas got it from Garrett and that it was probably shortened as a result of a bulge or ring in the barrel. A ring, or bulge results from a faulty round becoming lodged in the barrel and someone firing another shot, immediately behind it. It was more than likely shortened by an amateur gunsmith or similarly unqualified mechanic sometime after the Bacas got the gun from Pat Garrett. There would be no other reason to shorten a rifle to that length and limit the magazine capacity to approximately six rounds in lieu of its original seventeen. In any case the current owners claim to have extensive provenance on the gun linking it to Garrett. However, absent any reliable information to the contrary it would be unreasonable to discredit their assertions.[106]

Garrett also owned a Colt Single Action Army Model 1873 with a 7½ inch barrel in caliber .44-40 W.C.F. The gun has one piece wood grips and a blue finish. It is serial number 55,093, and is reported to be the one he used when he killed Billy the Kid. The pistol is in a private collection.

Prior to serial number 100,000 Colt numbered the cylinder and barrel of the Model 1873 with the last four digits of the complete serial number. After serial number 100,000 that process was eliminated. The serial number on the cylinder of this gun is 1,704. Somewhere along the line the original cylinder, which would have been marked 5,093, was changed. This practice is not unusual, but it would be interesting to know if it happened before Garrett shot Billy...or after.

Since Pat Garrett did not die until 1908 there are a number of guns that are claimed to have been owned by him in various museums and collections across the country. Although important collector's items, none are as significant as the Colt revolver Garrett used when he shot and killed Billy the Kid.

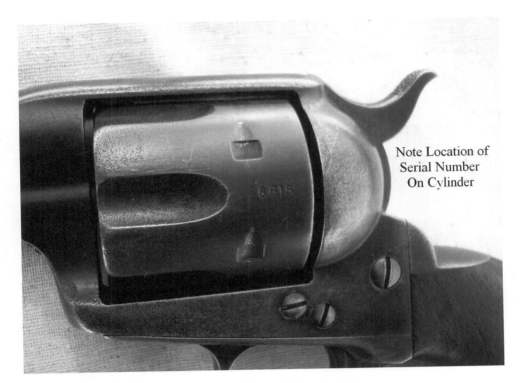

Note Location of
Serial Number
On Cylinder

Example of Serial Number on
Cylinder Colt Model 1873

11

The Guns Of Ameredith Robert "Bob" or "Pecos Bob" Olinger

*Fools live to regret their words,
wise men to regret their silence.*
—William Henry

Every story needs a villain. Thankfully Bob Olinger showed up in time to claim the title. Deputy United States Marshal Ameredith Robert "Pecos Bob" Olinger was born at Delphi, Indiana in 1850. Some have cited 1 April 1850 as his date of birth.[107] Sometime before 1860 his family moved from Indiana to Mound City, Linn County, Kansas. His father, William C. Olinger, died at Mound City in 1861. The family then traveled to the Indian Territory of Oklahoma where Bob remained for a brief time. Bob joined his mother and older brother John Wallace at Seven Rivers, New Mexico in 1876 and banded with the group known as the Seven Rivers Warriors, a notorious group of rustlers.

Both of the Olinger brothers fought on the side of the Dolan Faction during the Lincoln County War. After the conflict in Lincoln Bob killed a Seven Rivers Warrior named John Jones. Jones had killed Bob's good friend John Beckwith, who some believe may have been Bob's cousin.

Bob Olinger was a big man, standing six feet tall and weighing 240 pounds. He was known to be a bully, and was characterized as one by virtually all who knew him. Legend contends that his own mother is quoted as having said "Bob was a murderer from the cradle, and if there is a hell hereafter then he is there."

Bob Olinger was one of Bonney's guards at his trial at La Mesilla, and served as his jailer at Lincoln, where he is said to have constantly tormented Billy the Kid. On 28 April 1881 Billy escaped from the Lincoln County Courthouse. In doing so he shot and killed Deputy Bell and Deputy U.S. Marshal Olinger.

Bob Olinger had just bought a new Eli Whitney 10 gauge shotgun, declaring to all that he did so to use it to guard Billy. Billy used Olinger's gun to kill him with, firing both barrels at the unsuspecting Olinger from a second story window of the jail.

Events had come to a head that day. Billy somehow came to possess a pistol. There are several theories as to how he obtained the gun, none of which are believed by all and some of which are believed by many. Either someone concealed the gun where Billy could recover it, or he took it from Deputy James W. Bell after striking him over the head with his handcuffs. In any case, Billy was able to overpower Bell. During a scuffle that occurred at the head of the stairs Billy had no choice but to shoot Bell in order to make good his escape. He next picked up the new 10 gauge double-barreled shotgun that Bob Olinger had purchased exclusively for the purpose of guarding him and ran to a second story window of the jail. From his perch he caught sight of Bob coming across the street towards the courthouse. Bob had obviously heard the gunfire from the Bell shooting. As Olinger approached he saw Billy in the upstairs window. Billy greeted him with a cheerful "hello Bob." As Olinger approached, stunned by the greeting and seeing that Billy had the drop on him, he braced for the inevitable. Billy fired both barrels of Olinger's own gun through the upstairs window. Olinger tumbled over in a pile, most likely dead before he hit the ground. His chest, right side, and shoulder were peppered with eighteen wounds from the buckshot fired from the shotgun. Billy, still enraged at Olinger, broke the stock of the shotgun over the windowsill and tossed the pieces down on top of Olinger's body yelling, "damn you...you son of a bitch you won't corral me with that again." Some have contended that Olinger's gun was loaded with silver coins. From Olinger's postmortem report we know that claim is just one more of the many unfounded legends of the Lincoln County War.

As a Deputy United States Marshal one might question Bob's choice of shotguns. The Eli Whitney 10 gauge double barrel was far from the "gold standard" of firearms of the day. Eli Whitney was not a first tier manufacturer of quality firearms like Colt, Winchester or Ithaca. They were sort of a pedestrian firearm, and quite possibly one of the last choices a knowledgeable gunhand would have made if he or she had been there at the time. The Eli Whitney shotgun appears to have three triggers. There were two trigger guards. The rear one had two triggers, one for firing each of the two barrels. The front trigger guard had a trigger that operated the latch used to open the shotgun's action for loading. It was a very clumsy system, and frequently resulted in the weapon's operator thinking he or she was pulling a trigger to fire the gun when they were actually pulling a trigger to open the weapon's action. The result was that rather than firing, the weapon would literally fall to pieces in one's hands. One would think that a man like Olinger, who made his livelihood as a lawman, would have made a better choice.

In any case Billy the Kid shot "Pecos Bob" Olinger with his own gun on 28 April 1881 in the streets of Lincoln. Unfortunately the marker placed to memorialize the spot where Bob fell has his name spelled incorrectly, using two "L's" rather than one.

Marker Outside Lincoln Courthouse memorializing the spot where Marshal Bob Olinger fell dead.

Bob's Eli Whitney shotgun, which is serial number 903, was made in about 1874 and is in a private collection in Austin, Texas.

12

The Guns Of Billy the Kid

How history has treated certain characters is fascinating to observe. Often the common criminal, if he was charismatic, is more revered than its true heroes, if they happen to have been uninspiring.

Often what seems like the most unlikely character emerges as the hero of a historically significant incident. Such is the case with Henry McCarty, who by the time of his death was widely known as Billy the Kid.

At the risk of demeaning the character who so many find engaging, and believe to have been the pivotal figure of the Lincoln County War, Henry McCarty seems...on examination...to have been a rather poor choice when so many other candidates for the position were available. For reasons as different as the individuals themselves, many historians would have chosen Jose Chavez y Chavez, Richard Brewer, "Buckshot" Roberts, Charlie Bowdre or Jessie Evans long before Henry McCarty. Nonetheless, McCarty emerged as the designated hero and his legend has grown to epic proportion.

McCarty was, by all reliable accounts, a two-bit petty thief and cattle rustler when he arrived in New Mexico. Believed to have been born Henry McCarty he later went by the alias William Bonney and "Kid Antrim." The tabloid press created the name "Billy the Kid." He did not use that nickname until shortly before his death. He was thought to have been born around 1859-1861, perhaps in New York, Indiana or Missouri although the actual date and place remain a mystery. His mother's name was Catherine McCarty, an Irish woman, and his father's identity is unknown. The only accurate information known is that his mother was named Catherine and that she married William Antrim in Santa Fe, New Mexico and subsequently moved to Silver City, New Mexico. Henry had a younger brother named Joseph, who may actually have been a half brother. Some historians contend that Joseph was actually older than Henry.

After arriving in the Seven Rivers area of New Mexico late in 1877 McCarty immediately went to work as a cattle thief, and associated himself with the legendary Jessie Evans crowd. After several months he established a bond with John Tunstall, who Billy later claimed was the first man who ever treated him with dignity. This bond created great loyalty on the part of Billy towards Tunstall. After Tunstall's murder it seemed to have given Billy some sense of purpose.

Billy was known to have been an accomplished marksman. He was solely responsible for the killing of four people; Frank Cahill—done in self-defense, Joe Grant--done in self-defense, Deputy James Bell and Deputy U.S. Marshal Bob Olinger—done while escaping from jail in Lincoln. Legend attributes more killings to Billy than the aforementioned four men. Although he was involved in shootouts that resulted in the deaths of Bill Morton, Frank Baker, William McCloskey, William Brady, "Buckshot" Roberts and others there is no way to tell if it was his bullet that found the mark, thus making any claim of more than four killings an exaggeration. Further, the incident involving Joe Grant is the only true gunfight that Billy was ever involved in, and in that instance Grant's revolver was tampered with such that the first pull of the trigger would fall on an empty chamber. True, there were several desperate gun battles that Billy was involved in through the course of the Lincoln County War and, although fought to a mortal finish under grave circumstances, none meet the definition of a "face to face gunfight" done at close range and between two desperate men.

Nonetheless, Billy showed bravery and determination at various points during the several month long affair. Without question he displayed leadership during the twilight escape from the blazing McSween house.

According to legend Billy favored the Colt Model of 1877 self-cocking revolver in .41 Colt Caliber known as the "Thunderer." In his book *The Authentic Life of Billy The Kid* Pat Garrett claimed that Billy had such a gun with him at the time of his death. From what evidence and reference material that is available it seems that the Model 1877 was not the type

81

of handgun that he carried throughout the course of the Lincoln County War however. The only authenticated photograph of him depicts Billy carrying a Colt Model 1873 Single Action Army revolver. Legend has it that a man named Cherokee Davis, who worked as a cook for John Chisum, was given a new .41 Caliber Colt Thunderer by Chisum on 4 July 1881. When Billy rode into Chisum's cow camp along the Pecos he saw Davis's Thunderer and took an immediate liking to it. Billy proposed a temporary trade with Davis, which explains how Billy came to possess the Thunderer and had it with him when he was killed by Pat Garrett.

Some claim that Cherokee Davis lost the .41 Colt Thunderer somewhere along the line. There is, however, evidence that Davis sold the Thunderer to a collector named Maury Kemp in El Paso...and later sold Billy's Single Action Colt .45 to a doctor in El Paso. Both guns are now in the possession of private collectors and the provenance is though to be reliable.

Billy is said to have favored the Winchester Model 1873 carbine. He is also claimed to have been fond of the Whitney Kennedy carbine. In what is believed to be the only authentic photo of Billy he is holding a Winchester Model 1873 1st Model carbine and wearing a Colt Model 1873 Single Action Army revolver in a holster. The identity and whereabouts of the Winchester carbine has been lost to history.

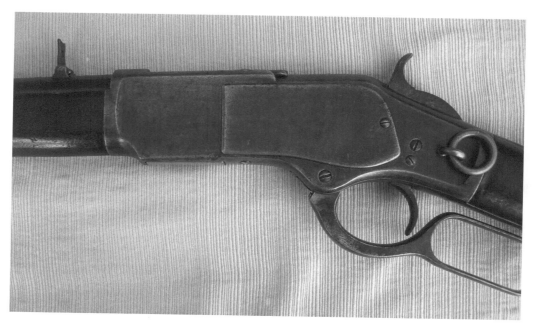

Winchester Model 1873 1st Model Carbine

Although Billy probably owned more than one handgun during the course of the Lincoln County War only one seems to have survived. That gun is a Colt Model 1873 Single Action Army revolver in caliber.44-40 W.C.F. with the barrel cut down to about 5½ inches. The pistol was reportedly taken from Billy on 21 December 1880 at Stinking Springs, New Mexico. The gun at one time belonged to noted actor William S. Hart. Hart died on 23 June 1946 at the age of 49 and the pistol is now in a private collection.

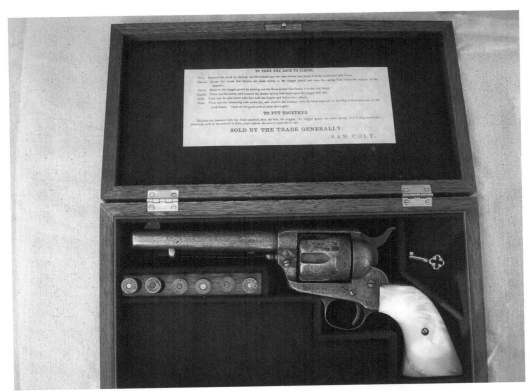

Cased Colt Model 1873 .44-40 W.C.F. with 5½" Barrel.

The young cowboy on horseback with the Montano Store in the background is believed by some to be Billy the Kid. The house across from the Montano store was the site of the Tomlinson's Drug Store. Tomlinson was a photographer, and may have taken this photograph.

13

The Guns of Sheriff William Brady

It is frequently a misfortune to have very brilliant men in charge of affairs. They expect too much of ordinary men.
—Thucydides

Sheriff William Brady was by no means the most dynamic person involved in the Lincoln County War. He may be the least understood, and the most misrepresented. Was he the evil villain so often portrayed, or simply an unwitting public servant acting upon the guidance provided by Lawrence G. Murphy and James J. Dolan?

William Brady was born on 16 August 1829 in Cavan, County Cavan, Ireland, son of John and Catherine (Darby) Brady. He attended school there and completed the required course of study by 1844, afterwards turning his attention to supporting his family. His father John died in 1846 in the midst of the potato famine, leaving William responsible for the wellbeing of his mother and siblings.

Brady left Ireland early in 1851, came to the United States and joined the army on 11 July 1851. He first served in Company "F," First Regiment Mounted Rifles. Brady's entire first enlistment was spent in Texas. He was promoted to the rank of sergeant in June 1855 and was discharged at Fort Duncan. Brady reenlisted on 2 June 1856 for another five year term, and was platoon leader of Company "F," Mounted Rifles, and was next discharged in March 1861 at Fort Craig. He then joined the New Mexico Volunteer Infantry on 19 August 1861 as a First Lieutenant and Adjutant. On 29 April 1864 he received his appointment as Commandant of Fort Stanton, and eventually assumed command of Fort Stanton on 14 May 1864. Although Brady never served with Lawrence G. Murphy, the two became extremely good friends.[108]

Brady was mustered out of the Army on 8 October 1866 as a Brevet Major (although some sources report the date as 31 October 1866).[109,110]

Soon after discharge Brady settled near Lincoln and staked claim to 1,000 acres of fertile land just four miles east of Lincoln. He purchased livestock and supplies from J. Rosenwald Company and William H. Moore & Co., all on credit.

Brady became sheriff in a close election on 6 September 1869. He preceded Saturino Baca and George Peppin as sheriff of Lincoln. The Irish born Brady was naturalized on 20 July 1869, thus barely receiving his citizenship papers by the time of the election. In the fall of 1871 Brady became the first elected official from Lincoln to serve in the Territorial House of Representatives. In spite of the fact that he was a Catholic, while in Santa Fe Brady became interested in becoming a Mason, and on 20 January 1872 joined the Montezuma Lodge. By 7 December 1874, he had risen to Master Mason status.[111] At the fall election in 1875 Brady again ran for sheriff and was elected, defeating Saturnino Baca.

On 16 November 1862 he married the widow Maria Bonifacia Chaves Montoya. Maria and William had eight children before he was killed, and Maria was pregnant with their ninth at the time of his murder. Claimed by some to be an ill tempered man when drinking, which by some accounts he did frequently, Brady is often portrayed as more of an evil man than might actually have been the case.

Most historians have judged Brady harshly, claiming that he willfully failed to take appropriate action in defense of the welfare of the community. Others have, treated him more evenhandedly, portraying Brady as a loyal, honest and honorable soul.[112] It has been inferred that Brady may not have been above average in terms of intellect. Nonetheless, there is no record of Sheriff Brady ever having killed anyone. For that matter he was never known to have treated anyone harshly, during his term as sheriff. But at the time of the Lincoln County War Sheriff Brady was a close ally of Murphy and Dolan, and heavily in debt, so his loyalty to them may have guided his actions.

Brady was killed on 1 April 1878 by a group of Regulators that consisted of Billy the Kid, Francisco Trujillo, Juan Trujillo, Anastasio Martinez, John

Scroggins, Oliver McElroy, Jerry Dillon, Henry Brown, Frank McNab, Fred Waite, John Middleton, and Jim French.[113] Bonney is frequently credited with firing the killing shot, but others have taken credit for the deed over the decades.

For decades historians have written about how Billy and Jim French made a mad dash into the muddy streets of Lincoln to retrieve Billy's Winchester rifle from the body of Sheriff Brady. Until recently the fact that the pair was unsuccessful in that endeavor has gone unmentioned. Among Brady's possessions at the time the postmortem, which was conducted by Mr. Thompson, was his Winchester rifle. This was the same gun that he had taken from Billy some months earlier. Judging by the serial number, the gun was made in 1874.[114] It is worth noting that Brady's Winchester seems to have disappeared from history and has never been seen again.[115]

Winchester Model 1873 Carbine 1st Model

Another fact that has been overlooked is that Brady was wearing a Colt Richards Model Conversion, serial number 150,210, at the time of his death. Based on the serial number range this pistol was manufactured around 1876.[116] The Richards Model was a cartridge conversion of a Colt Model 1860 Army percussion revolver done by the Colt factory. Brady's Colt pistol is in a private collection in New Mexico.

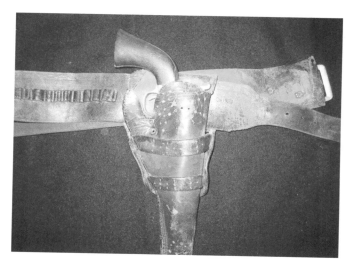

Sheriff William Brady's Colt Richard's Conversion.
Photograph provided by James Owen, Hobbs, New Mexico,
courtesy of the present owner.

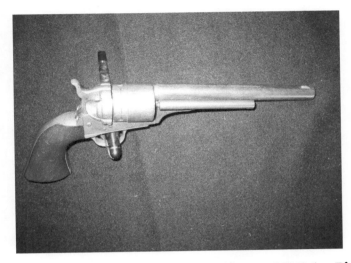

***Sheriff William Brady's Colt Richard's Conversion and Holster Rig.** Photograph
provided by James Owen, Hobbs, New Mexico, courtesy of the present owner.*

14

Where Did They Go?

We can be knowledgeable with other men's knowledge,
but we cannot be wise with other men's wisdom
—Michel Eyquem De Montaigne

One might ask what happened to all the valuable historical artifacts of the Lincoln County War that have not been accounted for? It seems that more of these guns would have survived, and be on display in museums or private collections. The plain and simple truth is that at the time of the Lincoln County War practically no one thought much of the whole affair, apart for those who were directly involved or impacted by it. Such conflicts, albeit not of quite as large a scale, were almost commonplace in the old west. Folks rustled your cattle, and you rustled them back. Someone wronged you...or took a shot at you... and you shot back. Generally speaking, guns were tools and horses were not often pets. When someone was killed, or lost a gun along the trail, the next man picked it up and used it until he was finished with it, then he passed it on. The guns, saddles, stirrups, spurs, chaps, holsters, cartridge belts, hats, cuffs, gloves and union suits were used up and discarded. Practically no one, apart from families who remained together, cared who the previous owner of their Winchester carbine had been. Their only concern was that it worked when it was needed.

Thus the trail of most of the artifacts of the Lincoln County War was lost long ago. A few guns did survive, largely by chance. Most did not. An amusing story comes to mind that a friend told me involving a pair of spurs that he bought from an old man down in the Rio Grande Valley of Texas. After his last horse died and he was unable to ride any longer the elderly gentleman, who had come to Texas from Mexico, tossed all of his old spurs that were lying around the tack room into a metal pail. The pail somehow managed to wind up along side an outbuilding where the rain from the roof drained directly into it. As a result all of the spurs in the pail were rusty or black. Two pair, however, were just heavily tarnished and when found were caked with mud. The two pairs looked alike, but one was smaller than the other. My friend bought both sets of spurs for around twenty dollars. When he got them home and cleaned them up he discovered that they were a rare, matched pair of men's and women's engraved, silver plated Garcia spurs worth thousands of dollars. Yes, such discoveries happen on rare occasions, but more often than not when someone at an antique store or an auction of cowboy collectibles hands you a Colt revolver that has "Billy The Kid" engraved on it one can be quite certain that it's not authentic.

There is an insatiable craving for all things cowboy. The quest, which reaches well beyond the bounds of the United States, has become so ferocious that unscrupulous individuals have resorted to fraud. Some are manufacturing collectibles, complete with what appears to all but the trained expert to be authentic old west provenance. These items continue to creep into the market place. Each year we old time collectors see more outlaw and lawmen guns than there were outlaws and lawmen! It's always humorous to me to see a pistol advertised as having belonged to a particular noted personality when I know the individual who owns the authentic piece, and know that it is locked up in his or her safe deposit box down at the local bank. Some of the relics that are held forth as authentic couldn't possibly be genuine, since they don't fit the period in history for which they are represented. I recently saw such a pistol advertised for sale by a woman in my own town. The nice lady claimed that her father had received the gun from a particular famed outlaw, whom she named. When I pointed out to her that the gun had not been manufactured until six years after that particular outlaw died she was not swayed in the least. Her belief that the piece was legitimate, in every way, remained resolute.

As the Englishman Thomas Tusser penned, "a fool and his money are soon parted." Take heed. If one wishes to learn about, and admire, the fine examples of firearms and accoutrements of the old west take a trip to a good museum.

Personally, I feel that there would be something magical about holding "Buckshot" Roberts' Winchester carbine in my hands. I have been studying and collecting guns of the old west since I was a thirteen-year-old lad and I have grown to accept the fact that I may never own a legitimate relic of that stature. But, don't stop dreaming and imagining the life and times of our childhood heroes. It is said that knowledge is power, but sometimes too much knowledge clouds our dreams.

As an ardent amateur historian and collector I have studied every minute aspect of the lives of my heroes, and in the end have occasionally turned my childhood visions to ashes. Find the knowledge and use it, but keep the dreams alive. If the most exciting vision one can conjure up is that of John Wayne portraying the aging U.S. Marshal Rooster Cogburn facing down a brace of bad men with grit and determination, and challenging them by saying, "...fill your hands you son of a bitch..." then keep that dream alive lest all this knowledge turn you into a bitter, disillusioned old grump.

Glossary of Terms

Bore: Synonymous with gauge, it is the numerical quantifier of the size of a shotgun

Breech: A part of a firearm located at the end of the barrel where the cartridge or charge of powder and shot are placed

Buntline, Ned: Pseudonym of Edward Zane Carroll Judson (E. Z. C. Judson) the dime novelist who commissioned Colt to make a run of long barreled pistols which he reportedly gifted to several notable lawmen.

Bullet: The lead or copper coated lead object that is spherical, conical, or flat topped that is propelled down the barrel of the firearm when the cartridge is fired, also called the projectile.

Caliber: The size of a bullet or cartridge measured in tenths and one hundredths of an inch.

Carbine: A shoulder weapon that is shorter in length than a rifle, and is generally designed to be used by persons on horseback. Favored for their reduced weight and maneuverability.

Cartridge: The small cylindrical vessel, generally brass, that contains the gunpowder, primer and projectile and is loaded into the breech or chamber of a firearm

Centerfire: A cartridge that uses a primer that is made separate from the cartridge itself and is installed in the center of the base of the cartridge body.

Chamber: The chamber of a firearm is the place where the cartridge is inserted. It is virtually the same diameter of the cartridge – but not necessarily the same diameter as the projectile.

Crimp: To press or pinch into small uniform folds, a means of attaching two objects.

Cylinder: The cylindrical part of a revolving firearm containing a number of chambers into which cartridges are inserted.

Derringer: Generally refers to a class of small, pocket firearms many of which are single shot and are intended for personal protection and are otherwise of little use as sporting arms.

Double Action: An operating action of a firearm that self cocks the hammer, and rotates the cylinder to a new chamber each time the trigger is pulled back.

Double Barrel: A firearm with two barrels mounted either side by side or one below the other. Generally, but not always, a shotgun.

Firing Pin: Generally pin shaped or a pointed, elongated rectangle it is the part of a firearm that strikes the primer—its impact thereon causing it to ignite.

Flintlock: A firearm having an operating action whereby a piece of flint held in the jaws of the hammer would strike the steel frizzen pan containing a small charge of gunpowder, thereby igniting the weapon.

Frizzen: Metal part of the action of a flintlock firearm.

Fulminate of Mercury: A primary explosive Hg ONC 2 is mercury, treated with nitric acid and alcohol which yields mercuric fulminate used as a primer in metallic cartridges.

Gauge: Measurement for calculating the size of a shotgun. For example, a 12 gauge means one can make 12 lead balls, each of equal diameter to the gun barrel, out of 1 pound of lead. Synonymous with bore, it is the numerical quantifier of the size of a shotgun.

Hammer: Moving part of a firearm that when allowed to travel forward when the trigger is pulled, strikes the firing pin and ignites the cartridge.

Handgun: A firearm that is held in ones hand as opposed to one that is intended to be fired from the shoulder, or from a stand or mechanism of some sort.

Lever Action: Generally a repeating firearm, a lever action firearm has a lever mechanism that opens the breech, loads a cartridge and extracts and ejects the spent cartridge while at the same time cocking the firearm for use—all in one complete up and down stroke of the lever.

Muzzle: The open end of the barrel through which the projectile leaves when the weapon is discharged.

Muzzle Loader: A firearm that does not use a cartridge, but is loaded with powder and shot or bullet through the muzzle end of the barrel.

Ned Buntline (See Buntline).

Pot metal: Any cheap, inexpensive alloy of metals generally poor in strength and tensile

Primer: A small, cup shaped object used to ignite gunpowder that is filled with fulminate of mercury or some other form of highly flammable material.

Projectile: Usually lead or copper coated lead, it is the object that is spherical, conical, or flat topped in shape andis propelled down the barrel of the firearm when the cartridge is fired, also called the bullet.

Rifle: A shoulder weapon.

Rifling: The grooves and lands that are machined into the bore of a barrel. They are machined at a slight twist so as to spin the projectile for improved accuracy. As the bullet expands when the weapon is fired it presses against the lands causing the projectile to spin as it leaves the barrel resulting in greatly improved accuracy.

Rimfire: A cartridge (or firearm using a cartridge) that uses a primer that is incorporated into the base of the cartridge and not a separate component part installed separately in the center of the base of the cartridge body.

Shotgun: A firearm that is designed to fire a paper, brass or plastic shell that contains a quantity of small lead pellets rather than a larger, single projectile.

Single Action: An operating action of a firearm that requires the individual to manually cock the hammer each time one wishes to fire the weapon.

Six-shooter: Slang term used by many to describe a six shot revolver, and often even more generally applied to any handgun used during the Old West era .

Smoothbore: A weapon that does not have a rifled barrel.

Trigger: Part of the firearm that one depresses to release the hammer in order to fire the weapon.

W.C.F.: Abbreviation for Winchester Center Fire, referring to a cartridge in a caliber that had been designed and introduced by Winchester for a center fire weapon.

Yellowboy: Nickname given the Model 1866 Winchester because of its receiver's appearance which is the result of the use of a bronze alloy called "gun metal" in its construction.

Dates of Manufacture

Colt Firearms
Manufactured Between 1874 and 1881

Conversions:

Thuer Conversion
The 1860 Army, 1851 Navy, 1861 Navy, 1862 Police, 1849 Pocket, 1862 Pocket Navy, 1855 Side Hammer and Dragoon
1868–1871 (Approx. 5,000)

Richards Conversion
The 1860 Army to .44 – serial number 1-8,700 and in percussion conversions 67,000 – 200,614
1873–1878 (Approx. 9,000)

Richards-Mason Conversion
The 1860 Army to .44 – serial number range 5,800 – 7,900
1877–1878 (Approx. 2,100)

Model 1851 Navy Conversions
.38 rimfire and centerfire from 1-3,800
1872 (Approx. 3,800)

Model 1861 Navy Conversions
.38 rimfire and centerfire from 1-3,300
1872–1878 (Approx. 2,200)

Colt Model 1873 Single Action Army Revolver

Year	No. Produced	Starting Number
1873	126	1
1874	2,599	126
1875	8,598	2,727
1876	11,825	11,326
1877	476	23,150
1878	3,872	23,629
1879	14,019	27,502
1880	22,015	41,522
1881	18,083	63,537

Colt Model 1877 Double Action Revolver

Year	No. Produced	Starting Number
1877	1	1
1878	3,000	2
1879	13,500	3,002
1880	19,000	22,021
1881	28,000	50,002
1882	34,000	84,002

Colt Model 1878 Double Action Revolver

Year	No. Produced	Starting Number
1878	1	1
1879	1,450	2
1880	4,000	1,452
1881	4,500	5,952

Colt Model 1878 Hammer Shotguns

Year	No. Produced	Starting Number
1878	1	1
1879	100	2
1880	2250	2,451
1881	7,850	10,201

Derringers

First Model Derringer .41
1870–1890 (Approx. 6,500)

Second Model Derringer .41
1870–1890 (Approx. 9,000)

Third or Thuer Model Derringer .41
1870–1890 (Approx. 45,000)

Winchester Firearms
Manufactured Between 1874 and 1881

Henry Rifle

Year	No. Produced	Starting Number
1860	270	1
1861	129	271
1862	999	301
1863	2,699	1,301
1864	3,999	4,001
1865	3,999	8,001
1866	1,999	12,100

Model 1866

Year	No. Produced	Starting Number
1866	2,337	12,476
1867	764	14,814
1868	4,189	14,479
1869	9,747	19,769
1870	23,010	29,517
1871	35,657	52,527
1872	21,599	88,184
1873	8,616	109,785
1874	6,636	118,402
1875	926	125,039
1876	5,941	125,966
1877	16,299	131,908
1878	2,285	148,208
1879	1,707	150,494
1880	2,177	152,202
1881	1,727	154,380

Model 1873

Year	No. Produced	Starting Number
1873	126	1
1874	2,599	126
1875	8,598	2,727
1876	11,825	11,326

Year	No. Produced	Starting Number
1877	476	23,150
1878	3,872	23,629
1879	14,019	27,502
1880	22,015	41,522
1881	18,083	63,537

Model 1876

Year	No. Produced	Starting Number
1876	1,429	1
1877	2,149	1,430
1878	4,387	3,580
1879	1,003	7,968
1880	5,728	8,972
1881	7,058	14,701

Shotgun Gauge to Bore Diameter Conversion Chart

Gauge	Bore Diameter (In Inches)
1	1.669"
2	1.325"
3	1.157"
4	1.052"
5	.976"
6	.919"
7	.873"
8	.835"
9	.802"
10	.775"
11	.751"
12	.729"
13	.700"
14	.693"
15	.677"
16	.662"
17	.650"
18	.637"
19	.626"
20	.615"
21	.605"
22	.596"
23	.587"
24	.579"
25	.571"
26	.563"
27	.556
28	.550"
29	.543"
30	.537"
31	.531"
32	.526"
.410	.410"

Popular Pistol Calibers
1874–1881 Era

.22 Rimfire
.32 Rimfire
.32 Colt
.32 Smith & Wesson
.32-20 W.C.F.
.38 Colt (Short & Long)
.38 Smith & Wesson
.38-40 W.C.F.
.380 Ely

.41 Colt (Short & Long)
.44 Rimfire
.44 Russian
.44 Smith & Wesson
.44-40 W.C.F.
.45 Schofield
.45 Long Colt
.450 Ely

Popular Rifle Calibers
1874–1881 Era

.22 Rimfire
.22 Extra Long
.25 Remington
.25 Stevens Rimfire
.25-20 W.C.F.
.32 Short & Long (also in Rimfire)
.38 Short & Long Rimfire
.32-20 W.C.F.
.38-40 W.C.F.
.40 Express
.40-50 Straight
.40-60 W.C.F.
.40-65 W.C.F.
.40-70 Straight
.40-70 Ballard
.40-82 W.C.F.
.40-90 Ballard
.40-90 Sharps
.44 Henry & Winchester Flat
.44 Rimfire
.44-40 W.C.F.
.52 Spencer Rimfire
.45-60 W.C.F.
.45-70 Government
.45-75 W.C.F.
.45-90 W.C.F.
.50-95 Express
.50-100 Express
.50-110 Express

Bibliography

Bonney, Cecil. 1971. *Looking Over My Shoulder, Seventy Five Years in the Pecos*. Roswell, New Mexico: Hall-Poorbaugh Press, Inc.

Klasner, Lily. 1972. *My Girlhood Among Outlaws*. Tucson, Arizona: University of Arizona Press.

Caldwell, Clifford R. 2008. *Dead Right, The Lincoln County War*. Mountain Home, Texas: Privately Published.

Cochran, Keith. 1992. *American West, A Historical Chronology*. Rapid City, South Dakota: Privately Published.

Cochran, Keith. 1994. *Colt Peacemaker Collector, Pocket Compendium*. Rapid City, South Dakota: Privately Published.

Coe, George W. 1984. *Frontier Fighter*. Chicago, Illinois: R.R. Donnelley & Sons.

Drummond, Douglas S. & Johnson, Rudolph H.. 2008. *Dr. William H. Elliot's Remington Double Derringer*. Santa Anna, California: Graphic Publishing.

Fulton, Maurice G.. 2004. *History of the Lincoln County War*. Tucson, Arizona: University of Arizona Press.

Greener, Graham. 2000. *The Greener Story*. London: Quiller Press.

Houze, Robert. 2001. *The Winchester Model 1876 Centennial Rifle*. Andrew Mowbray Publisher.

Jinks, Roy. 1977. *History of Smith & Wesson*. North Hollywood, California: Beinfeld Publishing.

Kopec, John A.. 1985. *A Study of the Colt Single Action Army Revolver*. Dallas, Texas: Taylor Publishing.

Madis, George. 1981. *The Winchester Book*. Ann Arbor, Michigan: Edwards Bros.

McHenry, Roy C. & Roper, Walter F. 1994. *Smith & Wesson Hand Guns*. Prescott, Arizona: Wolfe Publishing.

Mullin, Robert A. 1966. *A Chronology of the Lincoln County War*. Santa Fe, New Mexico. Press of the Territorian.

Nolan, Frederick. 1998. *The West of Billy The Kid*. Norman, Oklahoma: University of Oklahoma Press.

Nolan, Frederick. 1965. *The Life and Death of John Henry Tunstall*. Albuquerque, New Mexico: University of New Mexico Press.

Pirkle, Arthur. 2002. *Winchester Lever Action Repeating Firearms, The Model 1866, 1873 & 1876, Volume I*. Tustin, California: North Cape Publishing.

Supica, Jim and Nahas, Richard. 2006. *Standard Catalog of the Smith & Wesson*. Gun Digest Books.

Wilkerson, Don. 1998. *Colt's Double Action Revolver Model 1878*. Marceline, Missouri: Wadsworth Publishing.

Notes

1. Nelson, Morgan. "First Among Firsts, James Patterson, 1833–1892." *Wild West History Journal*. Volume II. Number 5. October 2009. p 3. Also see Kenner, Charles. "The Origins of the "Goodnight Trail" Reconsidered." *Southwestern Historical Quarterly*. Volume 77. January 1974.

2. Ibid. Also see op cit; Deposition of William C. Franks. 18 February 1898. Indian Depredation Case #5622.

3. Ealy, Glen Sample Phd. "Trading With the Enemy." *Texas Southwestern History Journal*. Volume 110.4. April 2007.

4. Knaut, Andrew L. 1997. *The Pueblo Revolt of 1680: Conquest and Resistance in Seventeenth-Century New Mexico*. Norman: University of Oklahoma Press.

5. J. Evetts Haley Interview with John Nichols. 15 May 1927. Lampasas, Texas: Haley Memorial Library & History Center. JEH.II.J1 and JEH.II.B (hereafter referred to as Nichols Interview).

6. Nolan, Frederick. 1994. *Bad Blood. The Life and Times of the Horrell Brothers*. Stillwater, Oklahoma: Barbed Wire Press. p 5

7. Ibid. p 105. Also see William Horrell service records. National Park Service. Civil War Soldiers and Sailors System. File M227. Roll 18

8. O'Neal, Bill. 1999. *The Bloody Legacy of Pink Higgins*. Austin, Texas: Eakin Press. p 27

9. Ibid. p 106

10. Ibid. p 106

11. John Nichols Interview. 15 May 1927. Also see Oz Nichols Interview. J. Evetts Haley Interview with John Nichols. 16 May 1927. Lampasas, Texas: Haley Memorial Library & History Center. JEH.II.J1 and JEH.II.B

12. Caldwell, Clifford R. 2009. *Guns of The Lincoln County War*. Mountain Home, Texas: Published by Author. p 1

13. Douglas, Claude Leroy. 2007. *Famous Texas Feuds*. Abilene, Texas: McMurry University. p 130

14. Tise, Sammy. 1989. *Texas County Sheriffs*. Albuquerque, New Mexico: Oakwood Printing. p 319.
    Shardack Thomas Denson was born on 1 February 1833 at Rankin County, Mississippi. He married Elizabeth "Betty" Sparks (21 June 1835 Cooksville, Mississippi, 1861) on 25 December 1851. The couple had six children: Frances E. "Fanny" (1853–1936), Albert (1854–1854), Samuel W. (1856–1939), Mary Cassandra (1858–1921), Sarah E. (1861–1941), and "Baby" (Unknown). Sheriff Denson eventually died of the wounds received, but not until almost twenty years later on 31 March 1892. Samuel W. Denson to L.R. Millican. Petaluma, California. 28 October 1930.

15. Nolan. *Bad Blood*. p 17

16. Ibid. p 17

17. The Texas Ranger organization between 1863 and 1873 was comprised of the Military, Minute Men and State

Police. The State Police organization was formed on 22 July 1870 and was dissolved and merged into the Frontier Battalions on 22 April 1873.

18. Sonnichsen, C.L.. 1951. *I'll Die Before I'll Run*. New York, New York: Harper & Bros. Publishing. p 97

19. Some accounts state that Williams had only four officers with him. See Nolan. *Bad Blood*. p 25. Also see Sonnichsen, C.L.. 1951. *I'll Die Before I'll Run*. New York: Harper & Bros. Publishing. p 97. Others indicate that Williams had seven state policemen with him. Information concerning the names of all eight Texas State Policemen was provided by historian and author David Johnson, Zionsville, Indiana.

20. *Norton's Union Intelligencer*. 29 March 1873

21. David Johnson to Clifford Caldwell. 9 January 2010. The remaining four Texas State Policemen were; Ferdinand Marshall, Henry Orsay, Sam Wicks and W.W. "Bill" Wren (not William R. 'Bill' Wren of Lampasas County). Also see Douglas. *Famous Texas Feuds*. P 131

22. Douglas. *Famous Texas Feuds*. P 131

23. Sonnichsen. *I'll Die Before I'll Run*. p 99

24. *The Daily State Journal*. 26 March 1873

25. Ibid. P 110. Also see letter from S.W. Denson to L.R. Millican. Petaluma, California. 28 October 1930.

26. O'Neal, Bill. 1999. *The Bloody Legacy of Pink Higgins*. Austin, Texas: Eakin Press. p 106.

27. Ibid. p 106

28. Ibid. p 27

29. Nolan. *Bad Blood*. p 29

30. Ibid. p 29

31. In *Bad Blood* Nolan cites the credit advanced as consisting of three loans: the first was $900 and was to be repaid on 1 March 1874. The second and third, totaling $3,762 each, were to be repaid on 1 August and 1 September 1874 respectively.

32. Frank Coe letter to J. Evetts Haley. 20 March 1927. Haley Memorial Library & History Center. Midland, Texas.

33. Dave Johnson to Clifford R. Caldwell. Manuscript dated 11 August 2011.

34. Jerry Scott was the former proprietor of the saloon by the same name in Lampasas, Texas.

35. Major Jon. S. Mason, Major 15th Infantry, Commanding Post Fort Sumner, New Mexico Territory letter. 25 December 1873.

36. Dave Johnson to Clifford R. Caldwell. 10 August 2011. See Interview of Elerdo Chavez by Edith L. Crawford, July 7, 1938, Federal Writer's Project.

37. Ibid.

38. *Silver City Mining Life*. 20 December 1873. See Dave Johnson to Clifford R. Caldwell. 10 August 2011.

39. Ibid.

40. *Santa Fe Daily News*. 29 December 1873. The *Santa Fe Daily Times* incorrectly reported the spelling of Sevenian Apodaca's given name as Levenian. U.S. Census Year 1870. Census Place Precinct 3, Lincoln, New Mexico Territory. Roll M593_894. Page 285B. Image 26. Also see Nolan. *Bad Blood*. p 91

41. Nolan. *Bad Blood*. p 91

42. Ibid. p 118. Also see Sonnichsen, C.L.. 1951. *I'll Die Before I'll Run*. New York: Harper & Bros. Publishing. p 101.

43. Douglas. *Famous Texas Feuds*. P 134

44. Ibid. p 123

45. Evans played a major part in the Lincoln County War and formed a gang called "The Boys." The Boys was a collection of ne'er-do-wells comprised of about thirty to forty outlaws, horse thieves and cattle rustlers many of whom had been members of the Seven Rivers Gang.

46. District Court Records. Dona Ana County, New Mexico (Las Cruces). Five replevin suits Case Nos. 368-72; larceny Case No. 449; and rioting Case No. 448. This information was obtained in 1926 by Maurice G. Fulton and is on file in the Chaves County Historical Society. See Hinton, Dr. Harwood P. "John Simpson Chisum". *New Mexico Historical Review*. Vol. XXXI July 1956 Number 3.

47. Nolan, Frederick. 1998. The West of Billy the Kid. Norman, Oklahoma: University of Oklahoma. p 75.

48. Thomas M. Yopp, relative of Wylie's foreman by the same surname, was born circa 1827 in Georgia. He lived to almost ninety-three, and died on 23 January 1920 according to his tombstone, however, other records indicate his date of death as 6 April 1920 at the Confederate Soldiers Home at Fulton, Georgia. Yopp is buried at the Westview Cemetery in Atlanta, Georgia. Yopp served as a Captain in the 14th Georgia Infantry, Confederate States Army. See National Park Service. Civil War Soldiers & Sailors Archives. File M226/67. Thomas M. Yopp.

   U.S. Census. Year: 1880. Census Place Precinct 4, Runnels, Texas. Roll 1324. Family History Film 1255324. Page 632C. Enumeration District: 111. Thomas Yopp, a relative of Wiley's foreman by the same surname, was still living with Wylie in 1880, working as a farmer. U.S. Census. Census Year 1860. Census Place Laurens, Georgia. Roll M653_129. Page 649. Image 153. Family History Library Film. 803129. U.S. Census. Census Year 1920. Census Place Edgewood, Fulton, Georgia. Roll T625_253. Page 2A. Enumeration District 168. Image: 979.

49. *The Santa Fe New Mexican*. 8 February 1877. Also see Fulton, Maurice G. *History of the Lincoln County War*. p 35-36.

   Thomas Benton "Buck" Powell was born in Mississippi on 24 July 1845 but was raised in Texas. He was a scout for General Shafter in campaigns against the Comanche Indians in 1869, and came to New Mexico in 1870 where he settled in the Seven Rivers area. Powell married Eliza Jane Hester, daughter of Rachel Carline Hester of Round Rock, Texas in about 1875. They had nine children. Powell was later involved in the assassination of John Henry Tunstall on 18 February 1878 during the opening phase of the Lincoln County War. In 1881 he shot and killed a man at Marfa, Texas. Powell posted bail but quit town and headed back to New Mexico. He died of natural causes on his ranch on the Rio Penasco 31 August 1906.

50. Some report this incident as having occurred on 10 March 1877. See Cramer. *The Pecos Ranchers in the Lincoln County War*. p 82

51. DeArment, Robert K. 2007. *Deadly Dozen: Twelve Forgotten Gunfighters of the Old West, Volume 1*.

Norman, Oklahoma: University of Oklahoma Press. p 116. In *Deadly Dozen* DeArment records that this incident occurred on March 10, 1877. All other sources seem to be in agreement that it occurred on 28 March 1877.

52. Mesilla Valley Independent. June 23, 1877. Also Coe. *Frontier Fighter.* pp 138-141.

53. Milo Pierce was born on 13 August 1839 at Lincoln, Logan County, Illinois. At the onset of the Civil War Pierce enlisted in the Second Regiment, Illinois Cavalry, Company B. He is claimed to have mustered out as a corporal in October 1865, but records seem to indicate that his unit was not dismissed until 22 November 1865. After the war, Pierce eventually headed west, arriving at Waco, Texas in January 1872. In the fall of 1873 he reached the Pecos River Valley and joined in a partnership with Lewis Paxton on a ranch below Seven Rivers. The following year he became one of the earliest settlers of Roswell.

Pierce maintained his partnership with Paxton until 1881. On 20 April 1882, he married Ella Lea Calfee, daughter of Joseph C. Lea. Shortly after his marriage he quit the cattle business and became a large scale sheep rancher, linking up with his father-in-law. In 1892 Pierce sold his sizeable ranch and began speculating in real estate. He also operated a significant meat market and butcher shop in the area. Milo Pierce died at Roswell on 20 October 1919.

54. James Highsaw Indictment. 10 March 1877. County of Dona Ana. Signed by Rynerson. On file at the Haley Memorial Library & History Center.

55. Grand Jury Record #451. Mesilla, New Mexico at the county seat at Dona Ana County. Signed by District Attorney William Rynerson.

56. Source reported to be David King of Wichita, Kansas. Susan Hollis to Clifford R. Caldwell. 6 July 2010.

57. Kelsey, Mavis Porrott Dr. and Kelsey, Mary Wilson. 1984. *Samuel Kelso/Kelsey, 1720-1796 : Scotch-Irish immigrant and revolutionary patriot of Chester County, South Carolina.* Houston, Texas: M.P. Kelsey. p 144.

58. Ibid. p 144.

59. Ibid. p 144.

60. Ownes was born on 27 May 1857, reportedly in Wales. He spent his early years at Cape Girardeau, Missouri before removing to Uvalde, Texas when he was about seventeen. At nineteen, he left home to join a cattle drive to Arizona. Considering the number of drives originating in the Rio Grande Valley, and the Texas Hill Country, during that period of time it is practically impossible to determine which particular outfit he was with, but Robert Wylie took a herd of 8,000 cattle to New Mexico in 1876 with Sam Coggin and Clay Parks. A Texas cattleman named Humphrey owned the cows, and they were to be delivered to San Carlos Apache Reservation. The drive started from San Felipe Springs, near present day Del Rio, Texas. Once in New Mexico Owen left the drive and went to work for Wylie. Owen remained in New Mexico for the rest of his life, and worked for Clay Allison of the Hash Knife Cattle Company. Along with maintaining a small herd of cattle on his own. He later worked with Milo Pierce. Jake and Milo built a rock house that was later sold to Clay Allison. After

Allison died the rock house was sold to John A. Haley, mayor of Midland, Texas. The four-room rock dwelling was at Pope's Crossing, and it was built in about 1880. Owen served as the second county clerk for Carlsbad between 1895 and 1908. Owen died at Carlsbad on 24 December 1939.

61. Fulton. *The Lincoln County War.* pp 37-38

62. Cramer. *The Pecos Ranchers in the Lincoln County War.* p 82

63. *Arizona Star* (Prescott). 13 July 1877.

64. In spite of continuing research Lawrence Gustave Murphy's origin remains something of a mystery. His obituary published in the Santa Fe newspaper on October 26, 1878, states that he was born in County Wexford, Ireland in 1831. It goes on to claim that he was educated at Maynooth College in Kildare, Ireland, and that he served United States Army at the rank of sergeant major. County Wexford has no record of his birth at that, or any other time. Maynooth College has no record of any student by that name ever attending that school. However, historian Charles Usmer has indicated that during a visit to the university he was able to locate evidence of Murphy's attendance. The Adjutant General of the United States Army has no record of any soldier by that name. Some believe that Murphy studied for the Episcopalian priesthood and came to New Mexico from Canada, although scant documentation exists to support this belief. He did not come to New Mexico with the California Column as has so often been written. The first known historical record of L.G. Murphy is dated July 27, 1861. On that date he was commissioned a First Lieutenant in the 1st Regiment of the New Mexico Infantry. He transferred to the New Mexico Cavalry and was with Kit Carson during the expedition against the Navajos and the subsequent relocation of the tribe to Fort Sumner.

Murphy was an excellent officer by all accounts and was eventually promoted to the rank of major for his meritorious service in the Navajo Wars and in controlling the Apaches at Bosque Redondo. In about 1868, in partnership with Lieutenant Colonel Emil Fritz who had been commander of the First Regiment California Cavalry, he established a brewery on the eastern edge of the Fort Stanton Indian Reservation. In the summer of 1870 the reservation was enlarged, and L.G. Murphy and Company became a privately owned island in the midst of government property. The partners made the most of their opportunity. In effect, they became both victualers (sellers of provisions to the military in the field) and Indian traders.

65. Some sources quote James Dolan's date of birth as 22 April 1848 while others cite 2 May 1848, which is the date that appears on his tombstone at the old Fritz ranch. In any case, he was born in Loughrea, County Galway, Ireland. Several years later his family immigrated to America, arriving in New York in 1854. Little is known of his early years. We know from his military discharge papers that he was only five feet two inches tall and weighed a slight 120 pounds. In 1863 he enlisted in Company "K" of the New York Zouaves (Zouave was the title originally given to certain infantry regiments in the French Army). In

1866 he reenlisted in the 37th Infantry and was eventually discharged at Fort Stanton in New Mexico Territory in 1869. Dolan immediately went to work as a clerk for Emil Fritz and Lawrence Murphy.

Dolan was a short, powerful and fearless young man. He was known to be dangerous when drinking. In 1874 Dolan was elevated to the status of "partner" in the Murphy store operation, and in 1877 Dolan and James Riley bought out the ailing Murphy and established J.J. Dolan & Co. Initially having no competition, Dolan grew rich by charging settlers and ranchers exorbitant prices for feed, livestock, and the basic needs of daily life. Dolan also controlled judicial and law enforcement officials in the area, and he maintained strong political connections with territorial governor William Axtell and Thomas Catron. After the Lincoln County War Dolan was charged, but never convicted of any wrongdoing in connection with his actions. On 13 July 1879, he married Caroline Fritz, daughter of Charles Fritz who owned the Spring Ranch. The couple had four children, two of whom died while still quite young. With the aid of Caroline's inheritance, he purchased the Tunstall ranch on the Feliz, moving his cattle there in 1882 when he made that place his home. He had also purchased the Tunstall Store in Lincoln. Dolan served as county treasurer from 1883 until 1888, and was then elected to the state senate, finally being appointed to the Federal Land Office at Las Cruces. After Caroline passed at the young age of twenty five, he married Maria Eva Whitlock in 1886. Dolan died at age fifty on 26 February 1898. He is buried at the old Fritz ranch, about eight miles below Lincoln on the east side of what is now Highway 380.

66. Pat Garrett, oldest son of John Lumpkin and Elizabeth Ann Jarvis, was born in Claiborne Parish, Louisiana, near Homer on 5 June 1850. On 25 January 1869 he left Louisiana and went to Dallas County, Texas where he worked as a cowboy from 1875 to 1877. Next he joined W. Skelton Glenn as a buffalo hunter in the Texas Panhandle where he killed Joe Briscoe in a disagreement (reportedly over buffalo hides).

On 7 November 1880 Pat Garrett was appointed Lincoln County Sheriff, taking over for Sheriff George Kimbrell who he had bested in the open election. His first goal as sheriff was to catch Billy the Kid. His posse tracked Bonney to the home of Pete Maxwell near Fort Sumner where, on 14 July 1881, Garrett shot and killed Bonney.

On 29 February 1908 he was shot to death while traveling to Las Cruces with Carl Adamson and Jesse Wayne Brazel.

67. The Minie ball is a type of muzzle-loading spin-stabilising rifle bullet named after its co-developer, Claude Etienne Minie. Minie's invention came to prominence in the Crimean War, and American Civil War. The Minie ball was a conical-cylindrical soft lead bullet, slightly smaller than the intended firearm's bore, and originally came with four exterior grease-filled grooves and a conical hollow at the base. When originally designed by Minie the bullet had a small iron plug in the base, its purpose was to drive the bullet forward and, under the pressure created by the ignition of the gun powder charge fill the hollow space and expand the lead skirting thereby gripping the barrel's rifling. The precursor to the Minie ball was created in 1848 by French Army captains Montgomery and Henri-Gustave Delvigne.

The bullet could be quickly removed from its paper cartridge and the gunpowder poured down the barrel followed by the insertion of the bullet which was driven in place by a ramrod. When the weapon was fired the expanding gas pushed forcibly on the base of the bullet, deforming it to engage the rifling. This provided spin for accuracy, a better seal for consistent velocity and longer range, and facilitated cleaning of barrel debris.

68. Fulminate of mercury is a gray crystalline powder, $HgC_2N_2O_2$, that when dry explodes under percussion or heat and is used in detonators and as a high explosive. See Reid, Alexander John Forsyth. 1955. *The Reverend Alexander John Forsyth and His Invention of the Percussion Lock*. Aberdeen University Press.

69. Born in 1766 Samuel Johannes Pauley was the son of a wagon maker. Pauley served as a sergeant major in the French Army, later adopting the unearned title of "Colonel." Pauley began tinkering with firearms, and produced a unique lock mechanism. In the process of doing so he recognized that the fulminate of mercury primer did not need to be in a separate mechanics, and combined the primer, powder and projectile into one full brass cartridge.

70. In February 1836 Colt patented their design in the United States, and on 5 March 1836, signed contracts with New York investors forming the "Patent Arms Manufacturing Company" of Paterson, New Jersey. The initial Paterson revolvers were sold from an office that was established in New York City. Small "pocket" pistols were offered in caliber .28, .31 and .34 with barrel lengths ranging from 2½" to 4¾". Mid-sized pistols with barrel lengths of 4" to 6"were available in .31 and .34 caliber. The larger "holster pistol" was available in .36 caliber only with barrel lengths of 4" to 12". The majority of the holster pistols had 7-1/2" and 9" barrels.

All Paterson revolvers were five-shot pistols, and featured a unique trigger that retracted into the frame and unfolded when the weapon was cocked. Most came with a separate loading tool, however in 1839 a fixed under-barrel loading lever was made available. In all, only about 2,850 Paterson Colt revolvers were manufactured.

Paterson Colt pistols soon found their way to the western frontier. One of the most well known users of Paterson revolvers was the celebrated scout Kit Carson. Carson wore a pair of Paterson's and fought Indians all along the Santa Fe Trail with them. Unfortunately for Colt, civilian sales of the Paterson firearms were not enough to keep the company financially solvent. In 1842 "Patent Arms Manufacturing Company" went completely out of business.

Prior to shutting the doors Colt supplied 180 of their .36 caliber Paterson Colt "No. 5 holster pistols" with 9" barrels to the Republic of Texas Navy. When the Texas Navy was disbanded in 1843 the Paterson Colt pistols were given over to the Texas Rangers, a militia unit assigned to suppress hostile Indians and bandits. Each ranger was issued two or three of the revolvers. See Silva, Manny. 2006. Unpublished Manuscript. Also see Madis, George. 1981. *The Winchester Book*. Ann Arbor, Michigan: Edwards Bros.

71. Oliver F. Winchester employed Benjamin Tyler Henry. On 16 October 1860, Henry was granted patent number 30,446 for a new rifle and ammunition. The 1860 patent had been assigned to Oliver F. Winchester but the guns were actually made on a contract basis by Henry, at the company plant at 9 Artizan Street, New Haven, Connecticut. In the process, the basic patent of 1854, held by Oliver Winchester, was also utilized. The new ammunition consisted of a copper casing .875 inches long containing the priming compound in the rim. It used a 200 to 216 grain bullet and 26 to 28 grains of black powder. This gave a muzzle velocity of around 1,125 feet per second. The Henry round gave about 568 foot pounds of muzzle energy. The copper cases were head-stamped with the letter H for Henry (see photo).

The gun itself held 15 rounds in a magazine beneath its 24 inch barrel. The rifle was loaded by turning the top five inches of the barrel housing. This gun when fully loaded weighed in at over 10 pounds. The Henry was advertised as some sort of super weapon with capabilities of hitting targets at 1,000 yards. What this rifle could do is to fire rapidly. Forty-five shots per minute could be attained. In other tests 120 rounds could be fired in 5 minutes and 45 seconds. See Madis, George. 1981. *The Winchester Book*. Ann Arbor, Michigan: Edwards Bros.

72. Kopec, John A.. 1985. *A Study of the Colt Single Action Army Revolver*. Dallas, Texas: Taylor Publishing. Also see Colt, S. (25 February 1836). Revolving Gun 9430X. *United States Patent Office Database*. United States Patent Office.

73. Jinks, Roy. 1977. *History of Smith & Wesson*. North Hollywood, California: Beinfeld Publishing. Also see Supica, Jim and Nahas, Richard. 2006. *Standard Catalog of the Smith & Wesson*. Gun Digest Books

74. Samuel H. Walker, Texas Ranger and Mexican War veteran, the son of Nathan and Elizabeth (Thomas) Walker, was born at Toaping Castle, Prince George County, Maryland, on 24 February 1817. Walker was the fifth of seven children. In May 1836 Walker enlisted in the Washington City Volunteers for the Creek Indian campaign in Alabama. After his enlistment ended in 1837, Walker remained in Florida as a scout until 1841. He traveled to Galveston in January 1842, where he served in Captain Jesse Billingsley's company during the Adrián Woll invasion. He then enlisted in the Somervell expedition, and took part in the actions around Laredo and Guerrero. Walker joined William S. Fisher's Mier expedition and escaped at Salado, was recaptured, and survived the Black Bean episode. In 1844 Walker joined John C. Hays's company of Texas Rangers and participated in the battle of Walker's Creek. During the engagement the rangers, using new Colt Paterson revolvers defeated about eighty Comanches. In April 1846 Walker formed his own company for duty under General Taylor.

Walker served as captain of the inactive Company C of the United States Mounted Rifles until the outbreak of the Mexican War. When the First Regiment, Texas Mounted Riflemen, was organized in June 1846, Walker was elected lieutenant colonel. He fought in the battle of Monterrey in September and on 2 October 1846, mustered out of federal service, activated his commission as captain of the mounted rifles, and proceeded to Washington, D.C., to begin recruiting for his company. There Walker visited Samuel Colt. Colt credited Walker with proposed improvements, including a stationary trigger and guard, to the existing revolver. The new six-shooter was named the Walker Colt. See Bauer, K. Jack. 1974. *The Mexican War, 1846–1848*. New York, New York: Macmillan. Webb, Walter Prescott. 1935. *The Texas Rangers*. Boston, Massachusets: Houghton Mifflin.

75. The Smithsonian Institute. National Museum of American History. Catalog #1993.0415.01. Accession # 1993.0415.

76. Wilkerson, Don. 1998. *Colt's Double Action Revolver Model 1878*. Marceline, Missouri: Wadsworth Publishing

77. Wilkerson, Don. 1998. *Colt's Double Action Revolver Model 1878*. Marceline, Missouri: Wadsworth Publishing. Judge Isaac Parker, often called the "Hanging Judge," from Fort Smith, Arkansas ruled over the lawless land of the Indian Territory in the late 1800s. In 1875, the Indian Territory (present day Oklahoma) was largely populated by cattle and horse thieves, whiskey peddlers, and outlaws who sought asylum in the untamed territory. The only court with jurisdiction was the U.S. Court for the Western District of Arkansas, located at Fort Smith.

Isaac Parker was born in a log cabin near Barnesville, Belmont County, Ohio on 15 October 1838. In 1859, at the age of twenty-one, he was admitted to the Ohio bar. He married Mary O'Toole, and the couple had two sons. Parker built a reputation for being an honest lawyer and a leader of the community. In 1868, he sought and won a six-year term as judge of the Twelfth Missouri Circuit. Parker arrived at Fort Smith on 4 May 1875 and replaced Judge William Story, whose tenure had been marred by corruption, At the age of thirty six Parker was the youngest Federal judge in the West. Holding court for the first time on 10 May 1875, eight men were found guilty of murder and sentenced to death.

Judge Parker held court a remarkable six days a week, and often was in session up to ten hours each day. He tried ninety-one defendants in his first eight weeks on the bench. During the summer of 1875 eighteen persons came before him charged with murder and fifteen were convicted. Eight of them were sentenced to die on the gallows on 3 September 1875. Only six were executed. One was killed trying to escape and a second had his sentence commuted to life in prison due to his young age. Parker was responsible for hanging seventy-three more convicted criminals between 1876 and his death in 1896.

78. Wilkerson. *Colt's Double Action Revolver Model 1878*. William Frederick "Buffalo Bill" Cody (26 February 1846–10 January 1917) was a legendary buffalo hunter, frontier scout, soldier, winner of the Congressional Medal of Honor, and later self promoter and showman.

"Pawnee Bill", born Gordon William Lillie (14 February 1860–3 February 1942) was an accomplished showman and self promoter, and in many ways emulated the style and format of William Cody's Wild West Show. In 1883 he was recruited to help coordinate the efforts of the Pawnee troupe in the first-ever Buffalo Bill Cody's Wild West show. Less known and less successful, Lillie invested in real estate, banking and oil while operating his wild west gift store and dabbling in motion pictures.

79. Supica, Jim & Nahas, Richard. 2006. *Standard Catalog of the Smith & Wesson*. Gun Digest Books. p 90
80. Ibid. p 93
81. Smith, Robert Barr. 2001. *The Last Hurrah of the James-Younger Gang*. Norman, Oklahoma: University of Oklahoma Press. p 168
82. Supica, Jim & Nahas, Richard. 2006. *Standard Catalog of the Smith & Wesson*. Gun Digest Books. p 94. Also see The Armchair Gun Show & Old Town Station News claims the following: "In the US, judging by photographic records and historical accounts, the rugged Colt SAA had an edge in popularity in the American West in the 1875-1900 era. The S&W had its partisans too, however. Among the noted individuals reported to carry one of the various S&W Model 3s were Frank and Jesse James, Buffalo Bill Cody, Annie Oakley, Texas Jack Omohundro, Dallas Stoudenmire, John Wesley Hardin, Charlie Pitt, Pat Garrett, Cole Younger, Bill Tilghman, Belle Starr, Frank McLowery, Theodore Roosevelt, and Virgil Earp."

Also see Samuel Hane. *Smith & Wesson #3:* "The top break Smith & Wessons were much more popular with the civilian population. The long list of notables on both sides of the law that favored the Smith & Wesson is amazing. Some of the outlaws are: Frank and Jesse James, Cole and Jim Younger, Charlie Pitts, John Wesley Hardin and Bob Ford. Some of the lawmen and scouts that favored the S&W are: Texas Jack Omohundro, Pat Garrett, Virgil Earp, Bill Tilghman, Dallas Stoudenmire, and Indian fighter Ranald MacKinzie of the 4th Cavalry."

83. Hane, Samuel. *Smith & Wesson #3:* The top break Smith & Wessons were much more popular with the civilian population. The long list of notables on both sides of the law that favored the Smith & Wesson is amazing. Some of the outlaws are: Frank and Jesse James, Cole and Jim Younger, Charlie Pitts, John Wesley Hardin and Bob Ford. Some of the lawmen and scouts that favored the S&W are: Texas Jack Omohundro, Pat Garrett, Virgil Earp, Bill Tilghman, Dallas Stoudenmire, and Indian fighter Ranald MacKinzie of the 4th Cavalry.

Also see James, Gary. "Smith's Forgotten Sixgun". 14 November 2008. *Guns & Ammo* – "On August 19th, 1895, pistolero, gambler, attorney-at-law, ex-con and all-around bad hombre John Wesley Hardin met his demise at the Acme Saloon in El Paso, Texas. Felled by a surprise shot from Constable John Selman's .45 Peacemaker, he never had a chance to reach for his .44-40 Smith & Wesson Frontier revolver. In what really amounted to an assassination by Selman, Hardin was blasted in the head at close range and then to make sure the job was done right, the lawman shot him in the chest and arm as he lay on the floor. Hardin's unfired S&W (serial number 352), along with Selman's Colt, were taken as evidence by the court during the investigation, and both guns were later sold for $100 by Hardin's nephew, Mannie Clements, to barman Tom Powers, where they were displayed in a shadowbox as featured exhibits at his Coney Island Saloon in El Paso for a number of years. As fate would have it, Clements himself would be gunned down at Coney Island in 1909..."
See Supica & Nahas, Richard. *Standard Catalog of the Smith & Wesson*. p 99

84. Supica & Nahas, Richard. *Standard Catalog of the Smith & Wesson*. p 99
85. Graham/Kopec/Moore. 1976. *A Study of the Colt Single Action Revolver*. Dallas, Texas: Taylor Publishing .
86. Drummond, Douglas S. & Johnson, Rudolph H.. 2008. *Dr. William H. Elliot's Remington Double Derringer*. Santa Ana, California: Graphic Publishers
87. Evans, Tim. *The Guns of Billy the Kid*. Varmint Media. John Tunstall's Forehand & Wadsworth British Bulldog pistol is currently on public display at the Ruidoso River Museum, Ruidoso, New Mexico.
88. Spellman, Paul N. .2003. *Captain John H. Rogers. Texas Ranger.*Denton, Texas: University of North Texas Press.
89. Madis, George. 1981. *The Winchester Book*. Ann Arbor, Michigan: Edwards Bros.
90. Goble, Paul. 9172. *Brave Eagle's Account of the Fetterman Fight*. London: MacMillan.
91. There is no record of what model Winchester Carbine Buckshot Roberts used at the Blazer's Mill fight. Since the date of that shoot out was 4 April 1878 he could have been armed with a Model 1866 or Model 1873.
92. Robert *McCubbin Collection*. Santa Fe, New Mexico.
93. Robert *McCubbin Collection*. Santa Fe, New Mexico.
94. Pirkle, Arthur. 1994. *Winchester Lever Action Repeating Firearms, Volume I The Models of 1866, 1873 and 1876*. Tustin, California: North Cape Publications. The author sites 63,853 as the total production of the model 1876. In Madis, George. 1981. *The Winchester Book*. Ann Arbor, Michigan: Edwards Bros. The author sites 63,871 as the production of the model 1876.
95. Madis, George. 1981. *The Winchester Book*. Ann Arbor, Michigan: Edwards Bros.
96. Christian Sharps was a native of Washington, New Jersey. Gun maker John Hall (1788–1841) at Harpers Ferry employed him, before he relocated to Cincinnati, Ohio, in 1844. In 1848 he patented his unique designs for a basic breech loading system, and created a single-shot rifle that used a linen or paper wrapped cartridge. In terms of function, after first lowering the breech block the user would insert the cartridge. As the breech was closed the end of the paper cartridge was sheared off, exposing the powder charge to the percussion primer. Sharps' design was simple and strong. In 1851 he formed the Sharps Rifle Manufacturing Company to market his firearms. Though Sharps himself resigned from the company in 1853, guns bearing his name become very popular. By the end of the Civil War the Union Army had purchased approximately 100,000 Sharps rifles. Later, the Sharps rifle became the preferred gun of buffalo hunters due to its power and

long-range accuracy. The Sharps system remains the basis for many single-shot rifles manufactured today.

Sharps left his rifle company and turned his attention to pistols, creating a .22 and .32 caliber rimfire metallic cartridge four-barrel pistol. His invention featured a hammer with a ratchet that revolved the firing pin by cocking and firing the four barrels in rotation. Before his death in 1874, Sharps had secured patents on more than fifty other inventions.

97. Caldwell, Clifford R. 2008. *Dead Right, The Lincoln County War*. Mountain Home, Texas: Privately Published. p 153

98. Marcot, Roy M.. 2002. *Spencer Repeating Firearms*. New York, New York: Rowe Publications. Christopher Miner Spencer (20 June 1833–14 January 1922) was an American inventor from Manchester, Connecticut. Spencer invented the Spencer repeating rifle, one of the earliest versions of a lever action repeating weapon. He also invented a steam-powered automobile and the first fully automatic turret lathe and screw machine.

99. Caldwell. *Dead Right*. p 136

100. The term "game getter" in this instance refers to a firearm used for the purpose of subsistence hunting...putting food on the dinner table. The term "Game Getter" is a registered brand mark of the Marble Arms & Manufacturing Company of Gladstone, Michigan. It refers to a Marble firearm that features a skeleton folding stock and a rifle barrel over a smooth-bore shotgun barrel. A manually pivoted hammer striker is used to select the upper or lower barrel. Three generations of the system were produced: First Generation (Model 1908), Second Generation (Model 1921) and the Third Generation currently manufactured by Marble Arms.

101. Greener, Graham. 2000. *The Greener Story*. London: Quiller Press. p 30.

102. Many accredited historians of the OK Corral incident claim that Doc Holliday carried a Belgium Meteor 10 gauge shotgun. The Meteor, made by Anciens Eslabissment Piper AKA Henri Piper became known as Henri & Nicolas. The gun had Damascus steel barrels. Pieper, Henri and Nicolas, Liege Belgium (Anciens Etabissments Piper) was founded in 1859. Piper's son reorganized the firm in 1898, and Henri left in 1905 to work on his pistol designs. The firm remained in business at least until the 1930s. Better known for the Piper pistols, the company also manufactured a wide variety of different types of shotguns and rifles.

103. Nolan, Frederick. 1965. *The life and Death of John Henry Tunstall*. Albuquerque, New Mexico: University of New Mexico Press. Also see Caldwell, Clifford R.. 2008. *Dead Right, The Lincoln County War*. Mountain Home, Texas: Privately Published.

104. John Henry Tunstall's Colt is on display at the Royal Armouries Museum in Leeds, HM Tower of London and is on loan from the Tunstall Family.
Forehand & Wadsworth Bulldog .455 Webley
Photo in Author's Collection

105. Gardner, Mark Lee. 2009 . *To Hell On a Fast Horse* .New York, New York: Harper Collins Books. pp 234-250

106. Staley Family. Provenance of the Pat Garrett Rifle:

According to family tradition, passed down over the past eighty years, the Pat Garrett rifle was acquired by W. W. Staley, Sr., a student at the New Mexico School of Mines, from Florentino Baca, also a former student from the School of Mines. Florentino Baca claimed a relative of his also named Baca and who was a 'famous lawman' had 'taken the gun away from' the famous Sheriff Pat Garrett. Staley and F. Baca were both students at the New Mexico School of Mines in Socorro, NM during the period; 1921 through the Spring of 1925 when Staley graduated. The 1920 U. S. Census of Socorro County, New Mexico enumerates Florentino Baca at age 16 living in the household of his maternal grandmother, Mrs. Sallie Berry in Socorro, New Mexico. Cipriano Baca served in the capacity of Deputy U.S. Federal Marshal under Marshal Creighton Foraker for most of Foraker's administration (1897 through 1912). During that period Cipriano regularly came in contact with Pat Garrett who was also a Deputy U.S. Federal Marshal under Foraker from 1897 until his appointment as a U.S. Customs Collector in 1901. Even after that time period, the two men must have met both socially and officially since both smuggling and border security were within the jurisdiction of the (Foraker) U.S. Deputy Marshals. Because the culture of law enforcement activities of those times required these men to develop a network of acquaintances that habituated the numerous saloons, bars and card rooms and because both men were known to gamble frequently, it is assumed the Pat Garrett rifle was acquired from Garrett by Cip Baca at the gambling tables, probably in El Paso, Deming or Las Cruces. Garrett was also known to be a frequent and persistent loser at cards, which eventually ruined him financially.

107. Thrapp, Dan L. 1991. *Encyclopedia of Frontier Biography*. Lincoln, Nebraska: University of Nebraska.

108. Muster Roll. August 1861. 2nd New Mexico Infantry. NA, RG p4. Also see Lavash. *Sheriff William Brady*. p 45

109. Nolan. *The Lincoln County War*. p 615.

110. Lavash. *Sheriff William Brady*. pp 20-28

111. Ibid. p 39. Also See Lodge Records. Montezuma Lodge. Santa Fe, New Mexico

112. Perhaps the most evenhanded account of William Brady can be found in Donald R. Lavash's book *Sheriff William Brady, Tragic Hero of The Lincoln County War.*

113. Haley Memorial Library & History Center. Robert N. Mullin Collection. Francisco Trujillo. RNM-VI-V.

114. Madis, George. 1981. *Winchester Dates of Manufacture*. Brownsboro, Texas: Art and Reference House. p 9.

115. William Brady's Winchester Model 1873, serial number 2,XXX, was manufactured on 16 September 1974. It was a .44-40 W.C.F. caliber rifle, with a 24" octagon barrel and a set trigger. See Cody Firearms Museum. Winchester Firearms Records. Factory order number 1,978.

116. Wilson, R.L. 1985. *Colt's Dates of Manufacture, 1837 to 1978*. New York, New York: Simon & Schuster. p 8.

Index

About the Author

Clifford R. Caldwell has continually cultivated his interest in western history since boyhood. After a stint in United States Marine Corps during the Vietnam War, and a successful thirty-five-year career working for several Fortune 500 corporations, Cliff is now retired and free to pursue his interests as a historian and writer on a full-time basis. Cliff holds a Bachelor of Science degree in business and is the author several books and published works including *Dead Right, The Lincoln County War; A Day's Ride From Here, Volume I: Mountain Home, Texas; A Day's Ride From Here, Volume II: Noxville, Texas; John Simpson Chisum, The Cattle King of the Pecos Revisited,* and his most recent works *Texas Lawmen 1835–1899, The Good and the Bad; Texas Lawmen 1900–1940; Robert Kelsey Wylie; Forgotten Texas Cattle King;* and *Eternity at the End of a Rope: Hangings, Lynchings, and Vigilante Justice in Texas.*

Cliff is recognized as an accomplished historian and researcher of the American West. He is a past member of Western Writers of America, Inc., the Wild West History Association, Texas State Historical Association and the Buffalo Bill Historical Center. Cliff and his wife live in the Hill Country of Texas, near Kerrville.

Printed in the USA
CPSIA information can be obtained
at www.ICGtesting.com
LVHW061931190124
769037LV00017B/105